Teaching Gerontology:
The Curriculum Imperative

Teaching Gerontology:
The Curriculum Imperative

Verle Waters, Editor

National League for Nursing Press • New York
Pub. No. 15-2411

This book was set in Goudy by Automated Graphic Systems. The editor and designer was Allan Graubard. Automated Graphic Systems was the printer and binder. The cover was designed by Lillian Welsh.

Printed in the United States of America

Contents

Contributors   **vii**

Preface   **ix**

Acknowledgements   **xiii**

1. Introduction   **1**
Mary Ellen Simmons

2. The American Nursing Home   **9**
Gail M. Cobe and Patricia Bentz

3. The Challenge to Faculty   **25**
Patricia Bentz and Janice R. Ellis

4. The Content Domain   **35**
Ann M. Carignan

5. Developing and Maintaining the Learning Environment   **55**
Mary Ann Anderson and Gail M. Cobe

6. What and How of Student Learning Activities   **65**
Elaine Tagliareni

Appendixes   **93**

Appendix A: Examples of Student Learning Activities with Well Older Adults   **95**

Appendix B: Examples of Fact Sheets to Assist Students in Integrating Gerontological Nursing Concepts   **107**

Appendix C: Sensory Loss Simulation Student Learning
Activity   121

Appendix D: Student Learning Activities for Examining
Attitudes Toward Aging   125

Appendix E: Student Learning Activities, for Functional
and Cognitive Assessment   129

Appendix F: Student and Faculty Discussion Guides:
Polypharmacy in the Elderly   141

Appendix G: Example of Objectives for Management
Experience in the Nursing Home   149

Appendix H: Sample Learning Activities: Ethical and Legal
Issues   153

Appendix I: Syllabus (Excerpt), The Nursing Home
Clinical   163

Contributors

Mary Ann Anderson, MS, RN, CNA, is Project Director, Weber State University, Ogden, Utah.

Patricia Bentz, MSN, RNC, is Professor and Project Co-Facilitator, Shoreline Community College, Seattle, Washington.

Ann M. Carignan, MSN, RNC, is Professor of Nursing and Project Director, Valencia Community College, Orlando, Florida.

Gail M. Cobe, MSN, RN, is Project Director, Ohlone College, Fremont, California.

Janice R. Ellis, PhD, RN, is Professor and Project Co-Facilitator, Shoreline Community College, Seattle, Washington.

Mary Ellen Simmons, MS, RNC, is Project Director, Triton College, River Grove, Illinois.

Elaine Tagliareni, MS, RNC, is Associate Professor, Project Director, Community College of Philadelphia, Philadelphia, Pennsylvania.

Verle Waters, MA, RN, is Dean Emerita, Ohlone College, Fremont, California, and Project Consultant, Community College-Nursing Home Partnership.

Preface

This resource and guidebook will help nursing educators revise curriculum to expand gerontological nursing content and develop clinical teaching opportunities in nursing homes. Although the experiences which gave rise to the ideas presented in these chapters took place in associate degree programs, nursing home nurses, educators in diploma and bachelor's degree programs, and graduate students will find useful and provocative ideas in these pages. Readers will find answers to the following questions and more:

- Why include gerontological nursing in the curriculum?
- Why use the nursing home for clinical education?
- What knowledge and skill should every AD program provide for students to learn care of frail older adults?
- What are the pros and cons of integrating gerontology vis-a-vis developing a separate specialized course?
- What learning experiences can be replaced or recast by adding gerontological nursing content?
- How can the learning environment in the nursing home be made suitable for students?
- What essential nursing content is best taught in a long-term care setting?
- How do learning outcomes differ between first and second year clinical experience in the nursing home?

These questions and the answers offered in this guidebook emerged in the course of a four-year demonstration project funded by the W.K.

Kellogg Foundation. The project, the Community College-Nursing Home Partnership, promised to show how associate degree nursing programs, dispersed throughout urban and rural America, could influence present and future care in the country's 16,000 nursing homes. A wide array of activities was undertaken at each of the six demonstration sites to meet the two major partnership goals: (1) to develop nursing potential in long-term care settings through in-service education and (2) to influence the redirection of associate degree nursing education to prepare graduates for roles in long-term as well as acute care settings.

In this guidebook we share what was learned in four intense and instructive years about clinical education in the nursing home and about gerontological nursing principles and practice in the associate degree nursing curriculum. Nursing teachers will find in these pages assistance with one or more of the following:

1. Assessing the appropriateness and adequacy of existing gerontological nursing content.
2. Modifying the existing gerontological nursing component of a program.
3. Identifying and developing new gerontological nursing content to add to a program.
4. Incorporating gerontological nursing content either by integration into existing courses or by adopting a new course.
5. Formulating a rationale for the nursing home clinical rotation.
6. Developing and fostering an effective learning environment in the nursing home.
7. Teaching creatively in the nursing home.

The six colleges participating in the demonstration project were:

Community College of Philadelphia
Ohlone College, Fremont, California
Shoreline Community College, Seattle, Washington
Triton College, River Grove, Illinois
Valencia Community College, Orlando, Florida
Weber State University, Ogden, Utah

In each of these colleges, the administrator of the associate degree nursing program served as project director, and all six stayed in the same administrative position for the grant and the nursing program for the full project period. The overall accomplishments of the project, including the work of the authors in developing this guidebook, is in part attributable to the stable leadership and commitment to project purposes of this administrative group:

Susan Sherman, MA, RN, Head, Department of Nursing, Community College of Philadelphia

Verle Waters, MA, RN, Dean Emerita, Ohlone College

Celia L. Hartley, MN, RN, Director, Nursing Program, Shoreline Community College

Carol Casten, MSN, RN, Chairperson, ADN Program, Triton College

Ann Miller, MA, RNC, Program Director, Nursing Valencia Community College

Gerry L. Hansen, EdD, RN, Director, Nursing Program, Weber State University

Special thanks also go to all of the faculty members in the six demonstration schools who helped to formulate, test, and put into practice the ideas about curriculum and teaching which follow. This project, like any change in educational practice, has not always been easy or unanimously endorsed. It is important to recognize that the achievements of the project are not the result of the work of a few individuals, but rather testimony to the creativity and collaboration of the faculty group in each college. In these six colleges, as in all good nursing programs, the curriculum represents the best thinking and hard won concurrence of the entire faculty.

Based on the success of the demonstration phase of this project, the W.K. Kellogg Foundation provided funding for an additional three years, from 1990–1993, to disseminate the lessons learned during the demonstration phase. A 17-minute videotape, *Time to Care: The Nursing Home Clinical,* has been produced and may be purchased from the National League for Nursing. The video addresses nurse educators as a primary audience and is a useful companion to this guidebook. The nursing teacher who is beginning to work with nursing home staff for purposes of developing a clinical placement will find the video helpful in clarifying and focusing educational objectives for clinical experiences in a nursing home.

Verle Waters, MA, RN,
Editor and Project Consultant,
Community College-Nursing Home Partnership

Acknowledgements

Helen Grace, Vice President, W.K. Kellogg Foundation, has been our project manager from the beginning. Her continuing support and belief in this project has made us work twice as hard to achieve the project purposes and objectives. We are deeply grateful to her and to the Foundation.

The National Advisory Committee for the dissemination project has assisted us in many ways: with good advice, sharing network connections, and cheering us on. We thank each of them for valuable contributions:

Sr. Rose Therese Bahr, PhD, RN, FAAN
Professor, School of Nursing
Catholic University of America

Richard W. Besdine, MD
Director, Travelers Center on Aging
University of Connecticut Health Center

Judith Braun, PhD, RN
Associate Administrator and Director of Nursing
Hebrew Home of Greater Washington
President, National Gerontological Nursing Association

James T. McCall, FACHCA
Consultant

Mathey Mazey, EdD, RN, FAAN
Professor, Division of Nursing
New York University

Robert E. Parilla, PhD
President
Montgomery College

Donna A. Peters, PhD, RN, FAAN
Project Director, Kellogg Project
In Search of Excellence in Home Care
Community Health Accreditation Program

Vera Reublinger, MA, RNC
Director, Professional Development Institute
American Association of Homes for the Aging

Leopold G. Selker, PhD
Dean and Professor
College of Associated Health Professions
University of Illinois

Joan Warden, BSN, RN, CDONA/LTC
President and Founder
National Association of Directors of Nursing Administration in Long-Term Care

And finally, we acknowledge our admiration and appreciation of Susan Sherman, Project Administrator and Head, Department of Nursing, Community College of Philadelphia. In the preparation of this book, the videotape, *Time to Care: The Nursing Home Clinical,* and all dissemination activities, she has facilitated our work in every possible way, forgiven our mistakes, and kept us moving.

Verle Waters

Teaching Gerontology:
The Curriculum Imperative

1

Introduction

Mary Ellen Simmons

DEFINITION OF TERMS

Discourse on the topic of nursing the older adult is complicated by a lack of clarity in language. Certain words are used interchangeably, others are avoided because of negative connotation, and some are favored because they imply a desired point of view. As faculty from the six demonstration colleges in the Community College-Nursing Home Partnership project began to work together, a need to define words and adopt consistent usage became apparent. A brief discussion of basic terms and definitions follows; any faculty undertaking curriculum discussions may wish to first clarify meanings and determine which terms best suit the faculty's intended outcomes.

Geriatrics is defined by Webster's dictionary as "a branch of medicine that deals with the problems and diseases of old age and aging people." The American Nurses' Association (ANA) established a Geriatric Nursing Division in 1966, and defined geriatric nursing at that time: "Geriatric nursing is concerned with the assessment of nursing needs of older people; planning and implementing nursing care to meet those needs; and evaluating the effectiveness of such care to achieve and maintain a level of

1

wellness consistent with the limitations imposed by the aging process."
This definition represented an important step for nursing by qualifying
the nursing of older persons as unique and different from the nursing of
younger patients.

Today, however, educators commonly reject use of the term *geriatric
nursing* on the grounds that it connotes a disease-centered, medically-
oriented view of health care for older persons.

In 1976, the ANA itself changed the Division of Geriatric Nursing
Practice to the Division of Gerontological Nursing in order to acknowledge the role nursing plays in the care of the healthy older person, as well
as the traditional role of providing care for frail and ill elderly. Here,
gerontology signifies the study of the phenomena of old age, and is inclusive
of medical, biological, sociological, and economic perspectives. Nurse
educators and authors prefer the terms *gerontology* and *gerontologic* because
they "denote the broad phenomena of the process of aging as encountered
in nursing education and practice." (Johnson, 1990, p. 1) Faculty members in the six project colleges also elected, after substantial discussion,
to use the term *gerontological nursing.*

The preference for *gerontological,* despite its all-encompassing meaning,
has prevailed over an effort by Gunter and Estes (1979) to introduce the
term *gerontic nursing* over a decade ago. They argue that the suffix *ology*
signifies "study of," and is not descriptive of the practice component of
nursing. They offer *gerontic nursing* as describing a service to the aged
which increases "health conducive behaviors," minimizes and compen-
sates for "health-related losses and impairments," provides comfort and
sustenance "through the distressing and debilitating events of aging,
including dying and death, and "facilitates the diagnosis, palliation, and
treatment of disease in the aged" (pp. 30–31).

Nonetheless, whatever their shortcomings, the terms *gerontological* and
gerontology are favored by educators and authors because they imply that
nursing's knowledge of aging and nursing services for older adults are not
limited to diseases. These are the terms that will be used in this guidebook.

When student experience in the nursing home first becomes part of
the curriculum, both students and faculty struggle to remember to call
the recipients of nursing home care *residents* rather than *patients* or *clients.*
The distinction is seen to be an important one since the nursing home
is the place of residence for most of the population being cared for.

Long-term care is defined by the American Academy of Nursing (American Nurses' Association, 1976) as "the provision of that range of services—physical, psychological, spiritual, social, and economic—needed
to help people attain, maintain, and regain their optimum level of func-

tioning." Long-term care has been defined as a set of health, personal care, and social services delivered over a sustained period of time to persons who have lost or never acquired some degree of functional capacity (Kane & Kane, 1987, p. 4). Both the Academy and Kane definitions encompass care in the home and in ambulatory service settings as well as in the nursing home. The phrase *institutional long-term care* is specific to nursing homes and like organizations.

Because the terms *long-term care* and *gerontology* shade into each other in common usage, discussions about the clinical learning activities of choice for instruction in care of the elderly are improved by first agreeing on definitions. There are significant differences as well as similarities between the nursing needs of the elderly in long-term care settings who are frail, dependent, and more or less stabilized and the nursing needs of hospitalized acutely ill older adults. Student experience in caring for ill older adults in an acute phase of illness is not a substitute for the experience of caring for frail, chronically impaired older adults in long-term care settings.

Searching for a term to describe older adults in need of nursing care encompassing both acute and long-term care settings, we have found *frail elderly* as satisfactory. *Frail elderly* is defined as: ". . . those old persons who have such social, economic, physical, or mental limitations that they need help from family, friends, or social agencies to perform ordinary tasks of living" (Yurick, Robb, Splev, & Ebert, 1980, p. 785).

A final term important to discussions about education and practice in gerontological nursing is *ageism*. Robert Butler (1981) defines *ageism* as

> *the prejudices and stereotypes that are applied to older people sheerly on the basis of their age. Ageism, like racism and sexism, is a way of pigeonholing people and not allowing them to be individuals with unique ways of living their lives. Prejudice toward the elderly is an attempt by younger generations to shield themselves from the fact of their own eventual aging and death and to avoid having to deal with the social and economic problems of increasing numbers of older people.* (p. 127)

Hidden ageist stereotypes lurk in the teaching materials and activities of most nursing programs, and it is the intention of the authors of this guidebook to prompt a conscious review of the total program.

WHY NOW?

It is only in the past few decades that the national health professional attention has been drawn on a heavy scale to the social, economic, political, and scientific questions of aging. Previously, while individuals may have lived into advanced stages of life, their numbers and proportion in the total population were not high. The late twentieth century, however, has witnessed a dramatic change in the number of citizens over 65, and in the length of the life span. Nursing always has been shaped by the population it serves; the clients under the care of nurses and the nature of their problems define the knowledge and skills required for practice. Every nursing teacher today knows that the aging of the population has affected health care services, and there is no lack of reminders from commissions, professional organizations, and nursing publications that the educational program must be revised to include more attention to the nursing needs of the elderly. But while the statistics describing the aging of the American population are indisputable, it is not clear nor is there agreement as to how this demographic reality should be reflected in the nursing curriculum.

To this date, the literature available to a nursing faculty for guidance in evaluating or initiating program content in gerontological nursing has been small in volume and general in nature. Bahr (1981) believes that until gerontological nursing is defined as one of the basic "specialties" required in every undergraduate curriculum, faculties will not push to identify essential content. Since 1981, Brower has addressed subject matter content and curriculum issues through a number of studies and surveys, (1981, 1983, 1985) and observes that "the complexity of curricular issues for the integration of gerontological nursing curricula may leave the timid or novice curriculum engineer in a state of despair" (1985, p. 75). Gerontological nursing content also is addressed by Gunter and Estes (1979) and Gioiella (1986). These authors, while identifying essential content for the baccalaureate and graduate program, did not include the associate degree nursing (ADN) curriculum in their studies.

With the start of the Partnership project in 1986, faculty in participating colleges reviewed background materials related to the didactic and clinical components of education for gerontological nursing. The complexities noted by Brower and the absence of published models for the ADN curriculum at that time challenged faculty to work together in establishing the domain of gerontological nursing content appropriate to the ADN curriculum. An approach known as DACUM (Developing a Curriculum) was employed to identify the knowledge and skill considered by practitioners essential to the nursing of elderly persons in long-term care settings. The results of that process and the judgement of faculty in the six demonstration colleges led to the content and clinical teaching ideas found in Chapters 4 and 6. A description of the DACUM process along with major outcomes also is found in Chapter 6.

WHY THE NURSING HOME?

As the following chapter describes in greater detail, the American nursing home has, for historical reasons, remained isolated from the mainstream of health care, and struggled to reconcile conflicting identities as welfare, health, and investment organizations. Nurse educators have not looked favorably on the nursing home as a clinical learning environment, except for the occasional nursing home placement of beginning students to practice elementary nursing skills. In recent years, however, the nursing profession has become more sensitive to the needs of underserved populations, including the residents of nursing homes. Newspaper and magazine articles periodically chronicle issues of care in nursing homes, and consumer action to expose and bring an end to questionable care practices has become usual. In this environment of changing consciousness and attitudes toward the nursing home and its residents' needs, more reason exists for a changed perspective on the relationship between nursing education and the nursing home. First, there is the responsibility of the educator to prepare graduates to care for the client population of the future. Second, there is the responsibility of the educational system in nursing to extend the benefits of educational affiliation to the nursing home, ending the deleterious isolation just mentioned which saps vitality and growth. Nurse educators and nursing home nurses have been strangers, estranged by history and by the biases and stereotypes that limit perception and opportunity. For these reasons the nursing home offers the clinical learning environment of choice when the curriculum purpose is to enhance education in nursing of the elderly.

WHY ASSOCIATE DEGREE NURSING?

The Partnership project, with its goal of redirecting associate degree nursing to encompass preparation for care of the elderly in long-term care settings as well as preparation for nursing roles in acute care hospitals, can be seen as a logical outgrowth of the history and mission of associate degree nursing. Founded in 1952 to prepare students to perform the role of registered nurse (RN), the associate degree curriculum has focused on the acute general hospital, where most registered nurses have worked. But curriculum in the community college is dynamic and pragmatic, with values and structures (in the form of advisory committees) that assure mindful attention to changes in the work world. As functions of the registered nurse role have changed in the decades since 1952, so has program content and learning activities.

Currently, the percentage of the RN work force employed in the acute care hospital is declining, the average age of the patient population is rising, and there is a growing demand for improved long-term care in community facilities, including the nursing home. The continuing increase in the demand for nurses in long-term care follows the shift of care delivery from hospital to homes and nursing homes, and it reflects a rise in minimum staffing requirements imposed by the state and federal agencies that authorize medicare and medicaid disbursements.

As the work place is changing so are the patients. In 1984, approximately one-third of the effort of a nurse was devoted to the care of someone over 65; today, unless a nurse chooses a career in pediatrics or obstetrics, two-thirds of his or her work life will be spent caring for patients over 65 years of age. The elderly have more illness, more chronic illness, and greater use of health services than other population cohorts. Of persons who turned 65 in 1990, according to a recent study by Kemper and Murtaugh (1991, p. 597), it is likely that 43 percent will enter a nursing home at some time before they die. The study indicates a significant increase in nursing home use over only a few years earlier. Of persons who died in 1986, only 29 percent had at some time been residents in a nursing home (p. 596). According to Dunkelman and Shore (1989, p. 3), there are now three nursing home beds in the nation for every two hospital beds.

The history of associate degree nursing demonstrates the ability of programs to produce significant numbers of nurses to meet changing health care needs of society. The need for registered nurses prepared to work with elderly in both acute and long-term care facilities exists now and will become ever more pressing. The Partnership project purpose of influencing the redirection of associate degree nursing to prepare graduates for long-term care as well as acute care is a necessity whose time has come.

Moving into the nursing home setting provided project faculty with the challenge to examine themselves as teachers and to rethink student–teacher relationships. In this guidebook, we have endeavored to share the insights and information which we found helpful to us as we inched toward meeting project objectives through work in our respective faculty groups to realize changes in the six programs. Faculty learned about the nursing home, its history, and the tortured circumstances of its existence today. As stated previously, nurse educators and nursing home nurses are strangers estranged by the past and by the biases and stereotypes that limit perception and opportunity.

SERENDIPITOUS OUTCOMES

The chapters that follow will elaborate three serendipitous themes that emerged from the faculty experience over the four-year project period. First, in addition to being an appropriate response to changes in society and health services, the clinical education in the nursing home is empowering for students and enlightening for faculty. Second, the nursing principles and practices essential for care of frail older adults in long-term care settings can be incorporated into the ADN curriculum, and strengthens rather than dilutes preparation for nursing in acute care settings. Third, the nursing home is a unique setting, and offers a learning opportunity for students distinctly and richly different than any other of the clinical learning environments. As a result, our perspective on the total curriculum has changed, and our view of the teaching role has been transformed. It is the hope of the authors that our words will tell the story.

REFERENCES

American Academy of Nursing (1976). *Long term care in perspective: Past, present, and future directions for nursing.* Kansas City: American Nurses' Association.

Bahr, Sr. R. T., (1981). Overview of gerontological nursing. In M. O. Hogstel (Ed.), *Nursing care of the older adult.* New York: John Wiley & Sons.

Brower, H. T. (1981). Teaching gerontological nursing in Florida: Where do we stand? *Nursing and Health Care, 10,* 543–547.

Brower, H. T. (1983). The nursing curriculum for long-term institutional care. In National League for Nursing, *Creating a career choice for nurses: Long-term care,* New York: The League, 45–64.

Brower, H. T. (1985). Knowledge competencies in gerontological nursing. In National League for Nursing, *Overcoming the bias of ageism in long-term care.* New York: The League, 55–82.

8 MARY ELLEN SIMMONS

Butler, R. N. (1981). *Aging and mental health.* St. Louis: C. V. Mosby.
Dunkelman, D. M., & Shore, H. A. (1989). Management in nursing homes. In P. Katz & E. Calkins, (Eds.), *Principles and practice of nursing home care.* New York: Springer.
Gioiella, E. C. (1986). *Gerontology in the professional nursing curriculum.* New York: National League for Nursing.
Gunter, L. M., & Estes, C. A. (1979). *Education for gerontic nursing.* New York: Springer.
Johnson, M. A., & Connelly, J. R. (1990). *Nursing and gerontology: Status report.* Washington, DC: Association for Gerontology in Higher Education.
Kane, R. & Rosalie K. (1987). *Long term care principles, programs, and policies.* New York: Springer.
Kemper, P., & Murtaugh, C. (1991). Lifetime use of nursing care. *The New England Journal of Medicine, 324,* 595–600.
Yurick, A., Robb, S., Splev, B., & Ebert, N. (1980). *The aged and the nursing process.* New York. Appleton-Century Crofts.

2

The American Nursing Home

Gail M. Cobe
Patricia Bentz

AS THE TWIG IS BENT

Nursing faculty, as others in the mainstream of health care delivery, harbor beliefs and feelings about the nursing home that are darkened by the shadow of its paradoxical history. Public policy and political decisions which have shaped the nursing home are different from those which created the modern hospital, and an understanding of the major historical influences promotes a more tolerant perspective. The last two decades have been years of dramatic changes in the American nursing home; by and large the public image and the attitudes of many health care professionals have yet to catch up with the improvements in care that have taken place, or with recent substantial changes in standards and minimum requirements imposed by regulatory agencies. In light of this situation, we will present a brief, and necessarily superficial history and description of the modern nursing home, in order that nursing faculty beginning a nursing home clinical rotation might understand, and be able to share with students, the background of certain idiosyncratic issues and practices encountered in the nursing home.

9

The predominance of proprietary ownership, the complex relationships with state and federal agencies, and the perceptions and misconceptions about nursing homes on the part of society at large all have roots in the tortuous history of this institution that Vladeck (1980) has called the "stepchild of both welfare and health policies" (p. 192). Many of the past political decisions and social attitudes affecting today's nursing home relate to its history as the descendant of nineteenth-century almshouses for the insane, the blind, the poor, and destitute elderly. The eminent Victorians believed in hard work and self-discipline as a means of overcoming any obstacle, and blamed those less fortunate for their own plight. Being poor, frail, and elderly was seen as moral failure. More than half the residents in poor houses were over 65 years of age, and most were seriously disabled. While eventually the call for more "moral" treatment of the mentally disabled lead to the state hospital system, the frail and disabled elderly were no better off there than in the poorhouse.

Not until the depression did the breakthrough in care for the elderly occur with passage of the Social Security Act. Old Age Assistance (OAA), passed in 1935 as part of Social Security, provided financial support for needy elders living in the community. But the appalling image of the poorhouse hung over the congressional deliberations, and not wanting to perpetuate the shame of the past, OAA benefits were specifically forbidden to any "inmate of a public institution." According to Vladeck (1980, pp. 36, 39), that exclusion planted the seeds of the coming growth of proprietary nursing homes, shaping the industry it would become.

The federal Hill-Burton Act, landmark legislation passed after World War II, supported the construction of hospitals in communities across the country. Primarily a program for the construction of acute care hospitals, funds were later allocated for the construction of not-for-profit nursing homes operated in conjunction with a hospital. Prior to that time, nursing homes were overwhelmingly residential and custodial in character. But with their incorporation into Hill-Burton, they were transformed, by definition, into medical facilities. To be eligible for federal funding, a nursing home had to meet standards of construction, design, staffing, and the like drawn by federal officials who were oriented to hospital construction. It was an orientation not suited to the purposes of the nursing home, and, in the view of many, it continues to be detrimental to the well-being of residents.

Proprietary nursing homes were not eligible for Hill-Burton capital funding. Stung by congress's exclusion of privately owned nursing homes, the organization representing the interests of that group, the American

Nursing Home Association (now the American Health Care Association) lobbied for federal support from other sources. Lobbying efforts were aided by a growing sense of need for expanding nursing home capacity, and federal assistance was gained late in the 1950s. When new legislation qualified proprietary nursing homes for loans from the Small Business Administration and the Federal Housing Administration, the doors were opened to large scale expansion of the nursing home industry as a business enterprise (Vladeck, 1980, pp. 44).

In 1965, Medicare was enacted. More than any other, this legislation transformed the provision of health care for the elderly. Initially it had little effect on the nursing home; the framers of Medicare were, in fact, unwilling to include reimbursement for nursing home care, which they saw as a bottomless budgetary pit. As hospital room rates rose with the expansion of technology and specialized services, however, fear grew that protracted hospital stays on the part of the elderly would constitute a great drain on the resources of Medicare. To avoid this, provisions were added for post-hospital care in nursing homes limited to a defined length of time. Medicaid, on the other hand, operated by the states, had a profound effect on the nursing home industry. Medicaid extended coverage to all medically indigent persons, and included services in "skilled nursing homes." Prior hospitalization was not a requirement, and large numbers of elderly with limited means became eligible. By the 1960s, the nursing home emerged as the dominant institutional setting for long-term care.

In 1968, the Social Security Act was amended to require institutions which receive funds from Medicare and Medicaid to undergo periodic inspections. These inspections, carried out by states as a condition of receiving federal funds, have become increasingly stringent over time. Since their inception, the regulatory inspections have been aimed primarily at improving nursing care and the quality of life for the residents in nursing homes, but until recently inspection standards focused on physical and procedural aspects of the environment and operation. In this regard, some in the nursing home industry argue that paper compliance and numbing restraint is all that has been achieved. However, most in the nursing home industry do agree that for a period the nursing home industry was not effectively policing itself and that government scrutiny did much to rectify substandard services.

The 1987 federal legislation known as "OBRA" (an acronym for the Omnibus Budget Reconciliation Act) contains a section entitled *The Nursing Home Reform Act*, which put in place beginning in 1990 a new set of regulations that will have, it is believed, a major impact on the quality of care in nursing homes. The 1987 OBRA legislation is seen as a turning point in the nature of assumptions made for the regulatory process governing nursing homes. (Willging, 1991). In the 1987 OBRA, there is new emphasis in the form of provisions for improving quality of care in nursing homes derived in large part from a 1986 study by the Institute of Medicine entitled *Improving the Quality of Care in Nursing Homes.* Included in the new regulatory requirements were standards which assume a relationship between the skills of those providing care and the quality of care:

- In-depth, uniform assessment of every resident (the Minimum Data Set, or MDS).
- Tools for measuring the quality of patient care.
- Improved training for surveyors.
- Increased staffings.
- Nursing aide training (Willging, 1991).

THE PLACES OF LONG-TERM CARE—
THE NAME GAME

Image concerns along with a steady shift away from custodial care to complex health care services have prompted a series of changes in the names given to the places where institutional long-term care is provided. The desire to escape the long-standing negative connotation of the name, *nursing home* (which actually replaced titles like *old age home* and *poor farm*) and to more accurately characterize the services provided, prompts facilities to call themselves *convalescent hospitals, health care centers,* or *nursing centers.* The variety of names given to the places where older persons are cared for in the community is expanded by Medicare and Medicaid, whose policies have led to classification systems for the varied populations needing long-term care and the types of living arrangements providing different levels of care. Many of the following categories are codified in state licensing systems for the approval of institutions providing care to dependent populations.

Sheltered Housing or *Assisted Living Settings* accommodate the physical limitations associated with the aged or the handicapped. Residents function without supervision, although communal meals and emergency call systems are usually in place. Some states now advocate making a social service worker available for residents on a need basis. Medicaid does not reimburse for care in sheltered housing, since no medical or nursing services are provided.

Personal Care Homes are also called domiciliary care facilities, residential care homes, or board and care homes. They provide room and board to persons who are essentially independent but require minimal assistance. The ability to be independently ambulatory is usually required, but some homes accept residents with canes, crutches, or walkers. Personal care home residents are not expected to require the services of registered or practical nurses, but some are connected to a skilled nursing facility which provides licensed staff for medications and treatments as needed. Medicare and Medicaid do not provide reimbursement for care in these care homes.

Intermediate Care Facilities and *Skilled Nursing Facilities* were, until the 1990 implementation of the 1987 OBRA, separate categories. The Skilled Nursing Facility (SNF, pronounced "sniff") received the bulk of the public funding. To be covered by Medicare or Medicaid, a resident had to require the supervision of a physician and the need for a registered nurse. Intermediate Care Facilities (ICF) were developed to serve people who did not require nursing services around the clock, but were too dependent for a personal care home. Since Medicare did not finance ICF care, economic incentives influenced the classification and location of residents, often in ways that were at odds with real needs. With the new nursing home legislation, officially these two levels no longer exist, although their names will undoubtedly continue to be used.

Nursing Facility (NF) is the new encompassing name now given in OBRA regulations for what were separately called the skilled nursing facility and the intermediate care facility. A single standard of care replaces the two sets of requirements.

Chronic Disease Rehabilitation Hospitals, or what are called *Subacute Units* in nursing homes provide a level of nursing services greater than most nursing facility residents require, but less than the level offered in acute hospitals. Patients are in a subacute unit for a limited time period. Respiratory support, intensive rehabilitation, and hospice are common services.

Each state both licenses and certifies nursing facilities, and each state has its own set of criteria. Licensing allows a facility to operate; certification provides eligibility for public funds. Nursing facilities apply for Medicare and Medicaid certification; they are not obliged to participate in either program. To be eligible for reimbursement from Medicare or Medicaid, facilities must meet requirements and specific standards. If a nursing home is consistently "out of compliance" (as revealed by the regulatory surveys), the government can and on occasion does terminate the "provider agreement" and refuses payment.

REIMBURSEMENT AND ITS IMPACT ON CARE

Medicare

Medicare pays for the care of more than 15 percent of all nursing home residents, although nearly 50 percent of all nursing homes are Medicare certified. Medicare limits its coverage to 100 days of skilled nursing home care per spell of illness, with full coverage for the first 20 days only. The nursing home admission must be within 30 days of hospitalization lasting three days or longer. Medicare further stipulates that it only supports services which are considered to lead to rehabilitation, and does not cover "custodial" or "routine" care. These strict federal requirements influence nursing care decisions where economic incentives may be different than the resident's particular needs.

Medicaid

Medicaid is the principal health care insurance for the poor, and it also is the principal source of payment for nursing home care. Eligiblity is determined by the resident's financial status, including all assets. The phrase "spending down" is used to describe the often painful and demoralizing interlude between marginal independence and eligibility for medicaid. Slightly more than half of all nursing home residents are covered by Medicaid.

Medicaid is a joint federal-state program; that is, the Social Security Act provides for allocation of funds to the states, with the state making direct payments to the nursing home on the resident's behalf. The per diem reimbursement rate paid to the nursing home on behalf of each qualified resident is set by the state. Physician services are paid for separately, and states determine which ancillary services are covered and which are not. Most states include nonprescription drugs, medical supplies, and physical and occupational therapy. Per diem reimbursement rates vary considerably from state to state. The reimbursement policies and procedures for this program are extremely complex, and the political tensions between providers, state officials, and advocacy organizations frequently focus on reimbursement rates and costs of care.

Other Forms of Reimbursement

More than a third of nursing home residents are covered by private insurance or individual and family financial resources. Health maintenance organizations (HMOs) pay for 12 percent of nursing home care, and the Veteran's Administration (VA) over 4 percent. Most residents exhaust their resources (spend down) in about two years, and then apply for Medicaid assistance (Marion, 1991).

THE RELATIONSHIP BETWEEN OWNERSHIP AND CARE

Nearly 75 percent of the nation's nursing homes are for-profit (proprietary) institutions, providing 70 percent of all nursing home beds (Marion, 1991). Proprietary nursing homes average 78 beds per facility; the voluntary not-for-profit homes are larger, averaging 98 beds if church-related, and 132 beds if public, or government-supported (Strahan, 1987, p. 2).

Forty-one percent of all homes or 50 percent of all beds are operated by multifacility organizations consisting of a number of nursing homes and called "chains" (Strahan, 1987, p. 2). The two largest chains, Beverly Enterprises and Hillhaven Corporation, have 9 percent of all beds (Marion, 1991, p. 9). Many of the facilities managed by chains are not owned by them, but are leased or operated under contract. In the past, high profits were achieved by some nursing home corporations largely as a result of real estate transactions. However, the economic climate of the late 1980s and the 1990s affected the nursing home industry, and profit margins were substantially reduced.

Church-related nursing homes account for 5 percent of all facilities and nearly 2 percent of all nursing home beds. Government (publicly) supported homes account for 6 percent of all facilities but over 10 percent of the beds (Marion, 1991, p. 8). Is there a relationship between the type of nursing home and the quality of care provided? Vladeck (1980) observes that "the few studies that . . . attempted to compare performance of proprietary and nonprofit facilities have found no statistically significant differences in the quality of care," and then goes on to say "based on my own observations and interviews . . . the average voluntary facilities are somewhat better than proprietary ones" (p. 123). The faculty members in the Community College-Nursing Home Project schools found in four years of working with community nursing homes toward the goal of developing effective learning experiences for nursing students that the "best" nursing homes had one characteristic in common: a sense of community among residents and staff. This sense of community derived from a variety of sources: religious affiliation, shared ethnicity or other group identity (for example, Masonic homes), small nursing homes in rural areas, or occasional urban homes with active ties to the surrounding community. In our experience, both for-profit and not-for-profit may exhibit this noted sense of community.

A SNAPSHOT OF THE NURSING HOME RESIDENT

The typical nursing home resident is 85 years old, without a spouse, female, and white. The chance of spending time in a nursing home increases with age; before a person becomes 75 the chances are 1 in a 100, but after 85 the chances are 22 in a 100. Sixty-three percent of nursing home residents have living children, and in contrast to the popular image of a population of older people abandoned by their families, most residents are supported and cared about by family members (Hing, 1987). Certainly, changes in modern life have altered the help patterns of adults toward their aging parents. The cohort now in nursing homes has fewer children than the earlier generations. The women who today might be caregivers for family elders are more likely to be in the workforce. There is one additional factor that is new: Because so many nursing home residents are very old, their children are themselves aged and may be facing chronic disability and diminished income.

Most residents resided in another institution or lived with community support of some kind before entering the nursing home. Many had lived with a family member for a period of time. For most, nursing home placement occurred after all other options had been exhausted. Seventy-five percent of residents are female and 93 percent are white. Only 6 percent are black and less than 1 percent are other people of color. The lower rate of nursing home use by non-Caucasion people may be a result of informal extended care systems within the community or other economic reasons, not discussed here (Hing, 1987, p. 2).

The average resident is more acutely ill than the average resident of a decade ago. He or she is older, and because he or she was in the hospital fewer days than was true before prospective payment practices existed, there is greater functional dependency. Most residents need assistance with the basic activities of daily living. In 1985, 91 percent of residents required assistance in bathing, 78 percent with dressing, 63 percent with using the toilet, 63 percent in transferring, and 40 percent with eating. Fifty-five percent of residents were incontinent of bowels, bladder, or both. Sixty-six percent of elderly nursing home residents were disoriented or suffered with memory impairment as a result of senile dementia (Hing, 1987, p. 4). In addition, more terminally ill people are now transferred from the hospital to the nursing home. Hospital deaths are declining, and nursing homes are now more than ever providing hospice services.

THE CAREGIVERS: NURSING HOME EMPLOYEES

The caregiver is central to all issues of care in the nursing home. More than location, building design, size, ownership, or licensure, it is the staff that residents value the most. But, lacking prestige, socially isolated, and besieged with economic woes, the nursing facility has difficulty finding and retaining competent staff. Most of the staff, primarily women, that are dedicated to this sector of the health care industry struggle gallantly with limited resources, wrestle with troubling ethical dilemmas, and deal daily with bureaucratic rules that emanate from distant government and corporation offices. Ethnicity, age, education, and social class of caregivers are all relevant factors affecting the social culture of the home and the resident's world.

Registered Nurses in Nursing Homes

Generally, the nursing community has not held kind thoughts about the professional competence of the registered nurse who works in a nursing home. In fact, it is our observation that the range of skill and ability among nursing home nurses is probably not very different from the range among nurses who work in acute care settings. In each of the demonstration sites we found effective nurses who choose the nursing home because it offers the opportunity to practice nursing in accordance with their values and desires. Fewer than 10 percent of registered nurses hold jobs in nursing homes, and most projections show an increase in that number over the next decade. Nurses in nursing homes are older, on the average, than nurses in acute care; the median age is 45 and most have worked in long-term care facilities for 10 years or more. Similar to the hospital nurse labor force, approximately 90 percent of RNs in nursing homes are white non-Hispanics; 56 percent are diploma graduates; 23 percent are ADN; 20 percent hold bachelor's degrees; and 2 percent held master's degrees (Strahan, 1988, p. 2).

Most nurses working in long-term care today have had no formal training in gerontological nursing. Prior to 1983, only 14 percent of nursing schools included specific curriculum content in gerontology. Until recently, nurses employed in nursing homes were isolated from mainstream nursing organizations and academic centers. For continuing education, they relied heavily on inservice programs that were prepared within the nursing home industry. Nursing home employers rarely paid for continuing education or travel to professional conferences or meetings, although in the 1990s that practice seems to be changing. Beset by paperwork, frustrated by regulatory and corporate demands, struggling to manage with scarce resources, and paid on the average 15 percent less than hospital nurses, long-term care nurses have not stayed long in any one job. Many move to another facility within commuting distance, looking for improvement in working conditions.

The Nursing Assistant: The Primary Caregiver

Nursing assistants (NAs) deliver 90 percent of the direct care in nursing homes, and represent nearly three-quarters of the nursing staff. Acknowledging their importance to the quality of care in nursing homes, the section entitled the *Nursing Home Reform Act* in the 1987 OBRA legislation included minimal standards for nursing assistant training. Each nurse assistant must complete a training and competency evaluation within four months of hiring in order to be listed on the state's registry. Once on the registry and certified, the assistant then must receive a minimum number of hours of continuing education per year.

Aides perform a wide array of services for approximately 10 residents on the day shift, 15 to 20 residents on the evening shift, and possibly

more on the night shift. The work is hard, and the compensation is close
to minimum wage. Women of color, unskilled and poorly educated, find
the nursing home a door to employment. Turnover in unexceptional
nursing homes is as high as 100 percent in a year. Greater stability in the
tenure of the assistant group is found in nursing homes where a community
of caring envelops both staff and patients. Many are drawn by the desire
for a job with human contact and the helper role.

"Overwhelmingly at the bottom of the American class structure . . .",
the personal world of the nursing assistant is far removed from middle
class culture. Most live in a subcultural ghetto, exposed to and burdened
with a life of economic and social hardships. Many must work two jobs,
are chronically stressed and tired, worry about child care, and may be the
victim of abusive parents or husbands or codependent in an addictive
relationship (Tellis-Nayak & Tellis-Nayak, 1989, p. 307). These workers
are the largest aspect of the social world of the nursing home resident. If
residents are to receive support and warmth, and are to be helped to feel
emotionally secure, then those who provide the bulk of the care also must
feel supported and secure. Nursing faculty who initiate a new clinical
learning program in the nursing home will be challenged to embrace an
educated perspective on this serious issue, and to allow students to grow
in their awareness of the social realities of modern American health care.

The Director of Nursing

The director of nursing in a nursing home is responsible for the organization and effectiveness of all nursing services. Regulations require that the
director be a licensed registered nurse, employed full time, employed by
only one nursing facility, and have administrative authority, responsibility, and accountability for nursing staff and services. The director's job
description includes implementation of the nursing home's policies, the
state's licensing requirements, certification procedures, and industry and
safety codes. The director is responsible for documentation, and is challenged to recruit and retain staff in a health setting with high vacancy
rates and high turnover.

The director of nursing is usually the most skilled, most visible, and
most available health care provider in the facility. Typically, the director
is supported by an assistant who is responsible for staff development and,
not infrequently, other duties as well. Without a medical presence, and
often without peer support, the director must be proficient in assessment,

identify clinical changes, and make decisions which frequently have
significant ethical and legal implications. The director is the touchstone
of relationships with family members, setting the tone and, more than
any other single person, setting the values, norms, and expectations
which govern care.

The Nursing Home Administrator:
Balancing Care And Finance

In 1967, the federal government published rules and regulations which
required each state receiving Medicaid money to establish licensing
requirements and set standards for nursing home administrators. Today
each state requires applicants to take both a national and a state examination in long-term care administration. Although the national examination is standard, state examinations vary, as do eligibility requirements
to take the exam. Administrators now holding that position have varied
levels of previous preparation, but the national standard, reflected in the
OBRA requirements, is moving toward a minimum of a baccalaureate
degree. Nearly all states require the completion of a practicum known
as the Administrator-in-Training (AIT) program. Preceptors for AIT
programs are nursing home administrators. Most, although not all, states
require continuing education for continuing licensure. Educational offerings are provided by the nursing home industry and its organizations.

The nursing home administrator may or may not have an ownership
interest in the nursing home, but the administrator is typically the person
most concerned with the bottom line of the financial statement. Along
with the owner or parent organization, the administrator sets guidelines,
establishes staff duties, and determines the pay scale. The administrator
is responsible for the home's survival, and that means seeing that regulations are met, financial reimbursement mechanisms are effective, and
that there is a successful marketing strategy. The administrator's knowledge and attitude have a critical impact in the nursing facility. Although
most administrators have a humane view of the elderly and the care that
is needed, they may be isolated from contact with the residents and the
day to day struggles of the staff.

Physicians in Long-Term Care: A Shadowy Presence

Every licensed nursing facility must have a medical director named as
responsible for the medical care delivered in the nursing home. Every

resident is required to have an attending physician. Almost half of nursing home residents use the medical director as their primary care physician; 57 percent choose their own doctor (Marion, 1991, p. 24). Nursing home medical directors usually see patients to approve treatments, to prescribe drugs, and to handle health problems that arise. The nursing staff deals with most patient care issues. While a large nursing home might engage a full-time medical director, more commonly a physician is affiliated with several facilities, and is reimbursed by each on an hourly basis. According to Marion, in 1990, the average medical director spent six hours a week seeing patients in the average nursing home (p. 24). Physician authorization is required for every admission to a nursing home, and for the first 90 days after admission the physician must see the resident every 30 days. After that period has passed, regulations require a visit every 60 days.

Physician education, like nursing education, has not been, on the whole, attentive to geriatric problems, and has not offered student experience with disabled elders in nursing homes. Medical care in the nursing home is different from other settings in that the goals of care, the clinical problems, the ethical considerations, and the available resources are all unique (Ouslander, 1989, p. 2582). Few primary care physicians have practiced in long-term care facilities, gained experience in treating cognitively impaired patients, made decisions where benefit-to-risk ratios are unclear, or practiced within a regulatory labyrinth. While formal training in geriatric medicine is now increasing, substantial change in medical services in nursing homes will probably not occur until the financial incentives improve.

The Licensed Practical Nurse

Licensed practical nurses (LPNs), called in Texas and California licensed vocational nurses (LVNs), outnumber registered nurses in nursing facilities. Facilities employ nearly 114,000 registered nurses as compared to 147,000 licensed practical nurses (Marion, 1991, p. 5). Church-related nursing homes have on the average 0.14 RN and 0.11 LPN staff per bed while for-profit homes average 0.6 RNs and 0.9 LVNs per bed (p. 25). With the exception of the director of nursing role, most facilities do not differentiate practice roles of these two levels, referring to them often as "the licensed nurses."

In general, the job market in long-term care has been less stratified than acute care, with resultant blurring of roles between RNs and LPNs.

In many facilities, licensed practical nurses have been hired or promoted into staff development positions; they are less costly to the facility, and less likely to move on. With the movement to upgrade the qualifications of faculty staff, there is a trend toward clearer distinctions and responsibilities between RNs and LVNs. Currently, there is pressure to require that the staff developer be an RN. As more registered nurses are prepared for care of the frail elderly, and take up positions in nursing homes, the benefits and responsibilities of differentiated practice must follow.

The Geriatric Nurse Practitioner

The GNP is a relative newcomer in the nursing home, and although it is claimed that the fully prepared practitioner can manage 80 to 90 percent of the health problems that beset nursing home residents, this role is still rarely seen (Ebersole & Hess, 1990, p. 767).

Educated in graduate or post-RN certification programs, nurse practitioners are certified following examination by the American Nurses' Association; some states have certification requirements as well. Typically, the geriatric nurse practitioner has four months of didactic instruction and eight months of clinical work with a preceptor. Programs are handicapped by the shortage of preceptors in nursing homes. Practitioners are prepared to take histories, perform physical examinations, order and evaluate laboratory tests, and to monitor and manage common acute, episodic, and chronic health problems (Ebersole & Hess, 1990). Empirical evidence suggests that when able to practice the role for which they were educated, they reduce medication usage, improve the functional capacity of many residents, decrease transfers to acute care, decrease emergency room usage, improve self-care, and increase staff morale and resident satisfaction.

The presence of the geriatric nurse practitioner in a facility appears to reduce costs to Medicare and Medicaid; there is, however, no evidence that costs are lowered for the nursing home. Without this latter incentive, few facilities are willing to take on an additional and high-salaried professional. GNPs now seen in nursing homes are more often part of a medical group owned and directed by a physician serving several facilities, rather than an employee in one facility with loyalties to its residents and staff. If the potential of the geriatric nurse practitioner in the nursing home is to be realized, their contribution to the care of residents will need to be demonstrated in clear and material terms.

CONCLUSION

Contemporary popular thought and even professional wisdom, to some extent, holds that there is a continuum of quality of care for dependent elders; on the one end the family is exalted as the caregiver of choice, and on the other, the nursing home condemned as the option of last resort. While alternatives to institutionalization need to be expanded, there always will be a large population of frail elders for whom residing in a nursing home will be the best option. We must remember that all elders *do not* fare better living with family members. Moving in with children may mean a move to a new community away from friends developed over a lifetime, to homes that have architectural hazards, with families in neighborhoods where adults are at work and children away all day, and in families inadequately prepared or reticent to provide the type of care needed. In addition to being at risk for social isolation, some elders have physical needs for assistance or supervision that cannot be met at home. Today's nursing home is designed to decrease architectural barriers which limit mobility, to provide a variety of activities that meet social and recreational needs, and to provide professional nursing care around the clock. In the nursing home, social and psychological needs are as important as physiological needs. Living is the active and central issue of care. Attention is focused on activities of daily living, rehabilitation for greater independence or maintenance, recreational and diversional activities, and support to families.

It is, however, a fragile balance. The negative effects of institutionalization are documented in literature of mental hospitals and nursing homes. Certainly, the nursing home has in the past been a place where individuals might be stripped of their identity, of their previously important roles and associated status, and where new identities were unwittingly and insensitively foisted upon residents. New OBRA requirements, intended to counteract precisely that influence, introduce new standards and language: "individual choice," "empowerment," "rights of residents," and "quality of life." For nursing students, the nursing home provides a unique opportunity to examine the differences between the impact of hospitalization in acute care settings and the nursing home. In comparing and contrasting the potentials and hazards of care in each setting, students can probe the role of the nurse and nursing care in altering the environment and creating an environment which supports living and dignified decline.

REFERENCES

Ebersole P., & Hess, P. (1990). *Toward healthy aging: Human needs and nursing response*. St. Louis: C. V. Mosby.

Hing, E. (1987). Use of nursing homes by the elderly: Preliminary data from the 1985 National Nursing Home Survey, *Advance Data* (No. 135). Vital and Health Statistics: National Center for Health Statistics.

Marion Merrell Dow Managed Care Digest: Long-Term Care Edition (1991). Kansas City: Marion Laboratories.

Ouslander, J. G. (1989). Medical care in the nursing home. *Journal of the American Medical Association, 262* (18), 2582–2590.

Strahan, G. (1988). Characteristics of registered nurses in nursing homes: Preliminary data from the 1985 National Nursing Home Survey, *Advance data* (No. 152). Vital and Health Statistics: National Center for Health Statistics.

Strahan, G. (1987). Nursing home characteristics: Preliminary data from the 1985 National Nursing Home Survey, *Advanced Data* (No. 131). Vital and Health Statistics: National Center for Health Statistics.

Tellis-Nayak, V. & Tellis-Nayak, M. (1989). Quality of care and the burden of two cultures: When the world of the nurse's aide enters the world of the nursing home. *The Gerontologist, 29*(3), 307–313.

Vladeck, B. C. (1980). *Unloving care: The nursing home tragedy*. New York: Basic Books.

Willging, P. R. (1991, May). *A strategy for quality assurance in long-term care*. Paper presented at the Ross Labs/National League for Nursing Invitational Conference on Long-Term Care. New York: Ross Labs/National League for Nursing.

3

The Challenge to Faculty

Patricia Bentz
Janice R. Ellis

INTRODUCTION

The challenge to community college nursing faculty is to respond to the demographic imperative of an increasing older population in a way that is consistent with the purpose and mission of the community college. How can this be done without compromising the intent to prepare a beginning generalist nurse? Can we teach the care of the older adult in the nursing home setting without slighting the needs of acute care settings for well-prepared nurses? Those who participated in the Community College-Nursing Home Partnership would say that the challenge is to balance these competing needs and demands creatively and effectively.

Because nursing faculty are aware of the aging of the population and aware of the community college's responsibility to respond to the needs of the community, few question the need for the inclusion of theoretical content related to aging. In fact, faculty no longer ask, "Should we include gerontology?" but "How do we integrate gerontological concepts?" The question that immediately follows is, "What content do we remove in order to add gerontology?" The answer, in large part, lies in how basic concepts already included in the typical associate degree nursing (ADN) curriculum can be presented differently. Stated another way, gerontology content can be the "vehicle" for teaching nursing rather than a "roadblock" of additional content. The next chapter will describe in detail how basic nursing concepts can be generalized to be inclusive of gerontological nursing practice. This chapter will offer suggestions for faculty development activities that support engagement in efforts to improve the teaching of nursing practice with older adults. When the Community College-Nursing Home Partnership project began in 1986, faculties in the six demonstration sites were hardly different from the average ADN faculty. Backgrounds in and attitudes toward gerontologic nursing in the curriculum were not unusual. Questions and issues identified here were raised by project faculty in early discussions, and the activities described below are those which were found effective in achieving desired changes in the curriculum.

Frequently, faculty respond to proposed expansion of gerontological nursing emphasis by saying, "Most of the persons we care for in the hospital are over 65—we don't *need* to go to nursing homes to find geriatric patients." While it is true that a large majority of patients in acute care settings are fragile older adults, student experience is different in the care-oriented nursing home setting than in the cure-oriented hospital unit. Using the nursing home as a clinical setting gives second-level students an opportunity to deal with rehabilitation, maintenance, and health promotion in ways that are not possible in the acute care setting, in part because hospital patient stays are now so short. The nursing home setting also gives the instructor the opportunity to interact with the student in a more planned and predictable way instead of in the hurried and sometimes crisis-oriented manner we do in acute care. In the acute care setting, we frequently interact more with the situation than with the student.

Furthermore, the shortage of nurses is even greater in nursing homes than it is in hospitals. Our graduates are not likely to make long-term care a career choice if they haven't been exposed to it and exposed to it at a level where they are able to see, experience, and appreciate the registered nurse role in the nursing home setting.

Another question faculty ask is, "How can we use the nursing home when there are such poor role models there? And the setting has so many flaws!" Our experience is clear that open expression and exploration of attitudes and opinions about old age and the nursing home is important. Feelings based on personal values and beliefs as well as actual experiences in nursing homes are useful discussion points. Students adopt the attitudes and behaviors of their instructors during professional socialization (Wilkinson, 1989), and attitudes are a legitimate component of curriculum discussion. Discussions might include questions such as the following: Are all nurses in acute care settings good role models? Are there no flaws in the acute care setting? How have we dealt with "imperfect" situations in the past?

PROMOTING INTEREST

We know there are faculty who have negative attitudes related to gerontology or the use of the nursing home setting for clinical practice. What can be done to engage faculty in evaluation of curriculum emphasis, in consideration of new teaching strategies, and exploration of new clinical settings? The inclusion of gerontological content, theoretical and practical, will be best accomplished if all faculty are involved, participating and contributing according to each one's area of expertise and interest. One approach is to bring in an enthusiastic expert, such as someone who has successfully changed courses and teaching strategies to better teach care of older adults. Enthusiasm is often contagious and has the potential to motivate and inspire others. Bringing in an expert to meet with a faculty group offsets the difficulty encountered when a single faculty member attends a conference and becomes excited about new approaches, but can generate no support or enthusiasm for change from colleagues upon return home. If all hear the same expert in the same setting (for example, at a faculty retreat), the enthusiasm may spread from one to the other.

Other faculty group strategies include having the faculty participate in a simulation game that offers a vicarious experience in coping with the struggles of old age, such as "Into Aging" (Dempsey-Lyle & Hoffman, 1991). An assignment similar to the "Well Elder" interview found in Appendix A-1 can be carried out by faculty and discussed at a faculty meeting. One or both of these exercises can be conducted with students as well.

PROMOTING INVOLVEMENT

The average faculty has a limited and dated understanding of the field of gerontological nursing practice. Its emergence as a nursing specialty is relatively recent, and even more to the point, the past decade has been marked by basic research in the sciences and a greatly expanded knowledge base for understanding health and illness in the elderly. While one or two members of the faculty may take on primary responsibility for course revision, new clinical experiences, and other program changes (Chapter 5 suggests criteria for selecting faculty to spearhead change, particularly in developing the nursing home as a clinical learning environment), the importance of total faculty involvement in curriculum change cannot be overstated. The challenge to faculty is to expand and update their basic knowledge of gerontological nursing in order to make well-founded programmatic decisions. In the six project sites, a variety of faculty development activities took place during the planning year before changes were instituted. Each program will have different needs and different resources, but the suggestions which follow may trigger ideas helpful to the reader. All of the following were successfully incorporated in faculty development programming at one or more of the six colleges in the demonstration project.

- Arrange for a specialist in gerontological nursing to make presentations or provide consultation to the faculty over a period of weeks or months.
- Commission an interested member of the faculty to identify resources and plan a series of faculty sessions at intervals over the period of a semester year including lectures, videotapes, focused discussions, or structured workshops.
- Identify outside conferences, workshops, seminars, etc., that are available and accessible for the next semester or the next year and support a systematic plan for faculty attendance with time allocated to reports and discussion.
- Identify learning opportunities available at the nearest federally funded Geriatric Education Center, and provide assistance to faculty for attendance.
- Reward efforts of faculty to obtain certification in gerontological nursing with time, money, trade-offs, praise, and recognition. Assist faculty member to obtain professional development funds.
- Provide faculty with resources: articles, books, bibliographies, videotapes, learning materials from other nursing programs. Create a special, accessible area for this collection.
- Identify one faculty member to collect, copy, and route materials to remainder of the faculty.

- Encourage faculty to get involved with educational programming in the nursing home.

Much of the above relates to faculty readiness for change. Your faculty may wish to review how they have responded to the need for change in the past and the implications that history has for the present. Fundamentally, we need to feel comfortable with gerontology and with the new setting as practitioners before we can be really creative about teaching.

FACULTY TRANSITION

Faculty need support as they move into new practice settings. It is essential to remind faculty that it takes time to build rapport and a sense of security in *any* new setting. Ask them to recall the last time they "pioneered" a new setting—even an acute care setting. If faculty have never worked or taught in the nursing home, expect them to be even more uncertain and uncomfortable.

Models of adaptation have been useful in examining human responses to various experiences. Examples include stress, death, and grief. It may be useful to use a "faculty transition model" to assist faculty to understand the feelings they experience as they move through the process of teaching in a new setting. We present two; the first was developed at the Community College of Philadelphia as experienced, full-time faculty moved from teaching assignments in the hospital to clinical teaching in the nursing home setting (Figure 3-1). Figure 3-2 (adapted from Brooke, 1989) also was adapted from a model of the phases nursing home residents go through as they adjust to the nursing home, after the observation by a project faculty member that the model, in addition, applied to the phases of adjustment for faculty new to the teaching environment of the nursing home. For the programs that applied the Brooke model to their own experience, it had the added advantage of teaching faculty about resident transition as they looked at their own.

THE COMMUNITY COLLEGE OF
PHILADELPHIA MODEL

Community College of Philadelphia (CCP) faculty entered the nursing home setting ambivalent and idealistic. They were ambivalent about the

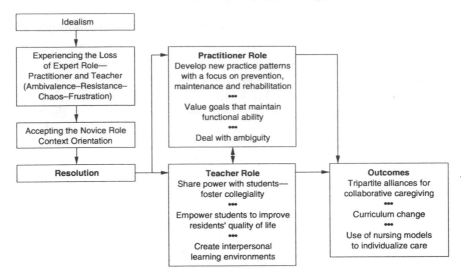

Figure 3-1
Faculty Transition to a New Practice Setting

value of the nursing home as a teaching site, but eager to share the expertise they felt in the planning of care and establishing standards of care. They were idealistic in that they felt they would be able to make a difference in this setting. However, faculty quickly realized that knowledge about frail older adults and a solid foundation in gerontological nursing theory was not sufficient to prepare them for the transition to teaching in the new setting. Gradually, faculty discovered that they needed also to understand the environment and culture of the nursing home, both being very different from the acute care setting. The old models for practice and teaching did not transfer intact to the new setting. As faculty found themselves outside their comfort zone, they began to realize that even as expert teachers they temporarily experienced a novice role. Unfamiliar with the best ways to teach in a setting with different goals and interventions. ". . . students are not the only novices; any nurse entering a clinical setting where she or he has no experience with the patient population may be limited to the novice level of performance if the goals and tools of patient care are unfamiliar" (Benner, 1984, p. 21).

Finding oneself in the novice role was frustrating, and the loss of the expert role gave rise to anger and resistance. But the gradual movement

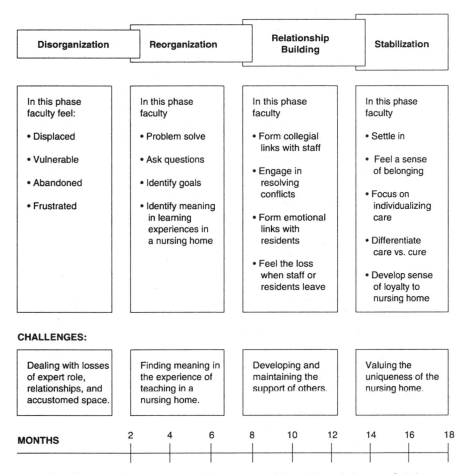

From V. Brooke (1989). Your helping hand: How to tailor your approach in each phase of adjustment. *Geriatric Nursing, 10.* Adapted with permission.

**Figure 3-2
The Brooke Model/ADN Faculty
Adjusting to a Nursing Home**

back toward a sense of being expert was accompanied by new and different ways of thinking, teaching, and interacting with students. For the faculty member, resolution of the tension occurred as new practice patterns with a focus on health promotion, maintenance and rehabilitation became clear. They began to value the role of the nurse in the nursing home setting as much as they valued the role of the nurse in the hospital. Resolution also occurred as a result of valuing the role of the teacher in the nursing home as much as they had valued the role of teacher in the hospital. New practice patterns resulted in new teaching strategies. Together, the new practice patterns and new teaching strategies led to a three-way partnership between instructor, staff, and students for collaborative caregiving, curriculum change, and individualized care. (Tagliareni, Sherman, Waters, & Mengal, 1991. See also Chapter 6.)

THE BROOKE MODEL

Brooke (1989) describes phases through which most residents pass while adjusting to life in a nursing home. Some faculty believe that the transition they experienced was similar and felt it was useful to share these phases with other faculty new to the nursing home setting.

The first phase, *disorganization,* is one in which faculty may feel displaced, vulnerable, and abandoned. They may feel a loss of expertise similar to the elder's loss of physical abilities. They also may experience the loss of relationships and "accustomed space" of the former familiar clinical setting. This phase is similar to the stage of assuming the novice role in the CCP model. The faculty may have difficulty seeing value in the experience.

To assist faculty during this phase, administrative and peer support is required to help faculty recover from a loss of confidence. The opportunity to spend enough time in the nursing home to become fully oriented and gain an understanding of nursing culture is helpful at this time. During *reorganization,* faculty begin to problem solve, ask questions, identify needs, and formulate a rationale for clinical education in the nursing home as they identify concepts that are successfully taught there. They begin to find value in the experiences available in this setting.

A suggestion to assist faculty during this time is to have them write goals for the experience, both personal and professional. This will help faculty to identify meaning in the nursing home experience. To the extent possible, we recommend that the instructor stay in one unit or section of the nursing home during this phase, coming to know it well before moving to another area.

Relationship building, and fitting in, although an ongoing process, truly happens when faculty begin to value the setting and the staff as making a significant contribution to the development of the nursing graduate the program desires. When this point is reached, the process of reciprocal support between staff and faculty begins. A member of the college faculty or nursing home staff who leaves is truly missed and a sense of loss is shared by both parties. In our experience this bonding process takes about six months. After the bonding occurs, collegiality exists between the professional staff and the instructor and the stabilization phase begins.

An interesting phenomenon occurs in the relationship between faculty and resident. Since staff turnover is often high, the most stable relationships developed by faculty may be with residents, who frequently remain in the setting over long periods of time. Faculty develop expertise about each individual's care requirements, and the likes and dislikes of residents. In some project programs, residents participate with students, nursing staff, and faculty in care conferences. Faculty may be actively involved in care planning and caregiving.

When the faculty member becomes established in the setting, *stabilization* takes place. Obvious signs that the stabilization process is occurring include an appreciation of the uniqueness of the setting as a place for student learning, courage to discuss concerns with the staff, an emerging loyalty to the facility, and valuing one's own position as a faculty member within the structure of the nursing home. During this phase, faculty gain insight into the uniqueness of each resident and his or her potential as a valuable learning experience for students. The focus on "care" versus "cure" becomes comfortable and the value of rehabilitation, maintenance, and prevention becomes apparent.

In conclusion, the challenges to faculty initiating teaching roles in nursing homes are many. The idea of giving increased emphasis to gerontological content may not be enthusiastically received by all. However, once successfully accomplished, the rewards to faculty, students, staff, and most of all, to residents greatly exceed the adversities encountered along the way.

REFERENCES

Benner, P. (1984). *From novice to expert.* Menlo Park, CA: Addison-Wesley Publishing Company.

Brooke, V. (1989). Your helping hand: How to tailor your approach in each phase of adjustment. *Geriatric Nursing, 10.*

Dempsey-Lyle, S., & Hoffman, T. (1991). *Into aging.* Thorofare, NJ, Slack.

Tagliareni, E., Sherman, S., Waters, V., & Mengel, A. (1991). Participatory clinical education: Reconceptualizing the clinical learning environment. *Nursing and Health Care, 12,* 248–263.

Wilkinson, J. (1989). Role modeling as a teaching strategy. *AD Nurse, 4,* 29–32.

4

The Content Domain

Ann M. Carignan

INTRODUCTION

This chapter offers specific ideas about essential gerontological nursing content in the associate degree (AD) program. In actual practice, each faculty decides for itself what the curriculum will be and the specificity of this chapter is not intended to be prescriptive, but illustrative. I will describe approaches found to be successful in programs participating in the Community College-Nursing Home Partnership with the hope that the ideas presented will enable readers to find new ways of enriching their own programs.

Currently, gerontological nursing content in the nursing curriculum is vaguely defined. A teacher or faculty committee beginning the task of identifying what to teach finds few guidelines for selecting the knowledge and skills essential for nursing practice. Concepts that make up the body of knowledge about aging needed for nursing practice derive from a number of disciplines: biology, psychology, sociology, medical sciences, and pathology. An expanding body of nursing literature provides some assistance to educators in determining what is most important to teach. But the decisions about what to select and what to emphasize, about balancing the time spent on normal aging and the well elder's health needs with time spent on the commonly occurring late life illnesses and nursing needs of patients, or about allocating clinical time to long-term care settings as well as acute care—are difficult. The question of whether to integrate gerontological nursing concepts in all courses or to develop a new, separate course may dominate a faculty discussion, with proponents on each side. Unfortunately, nurse educators have not as yet reached any normative standards for such decisions. Assessing the current status of nursing education and gerontology, a special committee of the Association for Gerontology in Higher Education noted the lack of requirements, standardization, or models for inclusion of gerontological content in the nursing curriculum (Johnson and Connelly, 1990, p. 4).

For some years now, the professional organizations have been involved in activities to motivate and guide nurse educators and enhance gerontological nursing practice. The American Association of Colleges of Nursing (AACN), American Nurses' Association (ANA), and National League for Nursing (NLN) have all sponsored mission statements and other publications defining essentials of practice and education. (AACN, 1986; ANA, 1982; NLN, 1988). Since the early 1970s, resolutions passed by attending members at conventions have repeatedly called for inclusion of gerontological content in nursing programs. At the 1989 NLN convention, an approved resolution, entitled "Gerontologic Component of Nursing Education," included as two of its three resolves:

> That NLN-sponsored conferences, workshops, and publications increase the attention given to topics related to gerontologic/geriatric nursing; and
> That NLN educational councils each undertake activities to enhance the gerontologic component of nursing education.

In 1987, ANA issued the Standards and Scope of Gerontological Nursing Practice, which provides a model for practice requiring a specific knowledge base about the older population.

GERONTOLOGY ACROSS THE CURRICULUM

Following the decision to increase the gerontological nursing emphasis in the curriculum, a dialogue begins about what the essential content shall be. A choice must be made between integrating new content into existing courses and establishing a new course with a specific gerontology focus. It is important that the faculty as a whole agree on what is important to teach and how the curriculum will change. Chapter 3 described the challenge faced by any existing faculty group that has traditionally emphasized acute care nursing. A nonconforming faculty member with an interest in long-term care nursing typically has been somewhat isolated, and although that faculty member might be left to do what he/she wanted to in his or her course, other courses were not influenced. Chapter 3 offers suggestions for promoting faculty interest and involvement. Our experience is that once the programmatic endorsement to adding gerontological nursing emphasis is made, faculty support and commitment evolves over a period of time.

Whether the faculty chooses an integrated or separate course design, there is a strong logical relationship between certain gerontological nursing content and core nursing concepts typically taught at different points in the student's program. In all six programs in the demonstration project, faculty found that while specific new content was added and curriculum design was modified in order to meet the goal of increased emphasis on gerontologic nursing, the major programmatic change over time was not in what was added, but in the focus and perspective on what was already being taught. An overview of different ways in which gerontologic nursing concepts were incorporated in nursing courses throughout the program will be followed by detailed examination of content topics.

Gerontology Content as Part of Fundamentals

Fundamentals courses introduce students to what might be called the curriculum's view of the recipients of nursing care. Concepts such as life cycle, human needs, stress/adaptation, or self-care are introduced as key elements. A hidden agist bias may exist in such courses if the case materials, videotapes, film, and written exercises all present the student with patient images that are young. (Gender and ethnicity may be similarly stereotyped.) Whatever the introductory concepts, they can be related to the elderly, and learning materials found or developed which convey to students a real picture of future patients. In introductory experiences with communication skills, purposeful interaction with a well elder also is a fruitful experience. As developed by faculty in one project school, and replicated in others, a learning experience in which the student meets with an elder at regular intervals has been effective. The learning focus is on communication skills, determining health needs in the areas of safety and nutrition, identifying stressors and coping mechanisms in grief and loss, and obtaining a life history. (See Appendix A for examples of student assignments.) The student thereby gains in understanding the phenomenon of aging. Complementing the clinical learning, lecture time is devoted to developmental needs of the older person and specific communication issues in caring for the patient who is older. Seminars facilitate student expression of attitudes, feelings, and reactions. Although students may initially feel anxious, as the relationship develops they become comfortable and involved. At Valencia Community College, the learning experience culminates with a class period in which elders and students meet together to examine salient features of their respective experiences.

Gerontology Included in the Study of Common Adult Health Problems

Typically, one of the first year nursing courses provides introductory "med-surg" theory and practice. The usual course outline identifies common health problems for which adults receive medical and nursing care. Gerontological content may be easily integrated into this curriculum. When gerontologic concepts are purposefully included, patient assignments can include specific opportunities to assess the physical and psychosocial changes of aging and their impact on the illness experience. Students compare and contrast the differences between young and old patients following surgery, analyze the impact of sensory deficits on a hospitalized elder, evaluate confusion related to physiologic disturbances, and identify differences in nutritional and elimination patterns.

At Community College of Philadelphia faculty members with advanced preparation in gerontological nursing piloted the use of what were called "Fact Sheets," prepared and distributed to other faculty members to assist them in integrating gerontologic concepts into their courses. In a short period of time the fact sheets were adapted for distribution to students to assist *them* in integrating gerontologic concepts. The use of fact sheets was quickly adopted by several other project faculties as well. (Examples are found in Appendix B.)

This period, when students are attending to the effects of age-related changes on the illness experience, is a propitious time to engage them in an experiential exercise that focuses on sensorial/perceptual disturbances (for example, see Appendix C).

At Valencia Community College and Triton College, students spend a day in an adult day care setting, a home visit, or in the office of a physician with a large geriatric practice. Students learn about services available to the chronically ill aged by completing a functional assessment of the client, and identifying the services appropriate to maintaining independence. The ability to assess functional status, identify health care goals in chronic illness, and cite community resources will be applied as well to experiences the students will have later in acute and long-term care institutional settings. The day or home care experience provides a transition between the first semester experience with a well elder and later assignments to provide comprehensive care for a hospitalized older patient. The continuum of care also can be included to emphasize community resources related to health promotion, restoration, and rehabilitation.

Gerontology Content Exemplifies Complex Adult Health Problems

In an ADN curriculum, students normally enroll in a third or fourth semester course emphasizing the care of adults with complex nursing needs. As part of this course, or in a separate course offered in proximity to it, project schools have allocated three to four weeks of clinical assignment to a nursing home experience. The contrast between the care of older adults in acute settings and those in long-term care settings provides a valuable learning experience. Understanding the physiologic conditions which produce confusion in the elderly, recognizing subtle changes in patient condition, sensitivity to medication management—these abilities and others are cultivated by the opportunity to be with patients in both settings. Chapter 6 provides greater detail about designing clinical experience in the nursing home to teach rehabilitation, management of the environment, leadership skills, and assessment.

Gerontology Has a Cameo Role in Maternal and Child Health (MCH)

Although most emphasis in the MCH course or courses obviously remains on the childbearing and childrearing family, assignments can be added specific to the grandparenting role and the special needs of families where small children and dependent elders are both in the home. Interviews with grandparents have been a fruitful assignment, and students have been asked to include a component in a care plan assignment reflecting the involvement of grandparents in the birth and early care of a grandchild. In curricula where women's health care issues are included in the Maternal-Child Health course, as at Shoreline Community College, concerns and problems of the older woman can be addressed.

As a Component of Mental Health Nursing

This course can be the ideal time, and the nursing home can be the ideal setting, for experiences designed to assist the student in assessing the degree to which the older adult has met the developmental tasks of aging. Students can identify adaptive mechanisms used by individuals as they adjust to retirement, to loss of loved ones, and to changes in activities, roles, and living arrangements. In one program, students have a 1:1 experience over a 10-week period during which they focus on a relationship with an older adult; some are well adults and others have a degree of dementia or other mental disorder. Students assess cognitive ability, body image, attitudes toward life experience, and evaluate the effect of chronic illness on each of these.

The nursing home experience provides students an unparalleled opportunity to differentiate between delirium, depression, and dementia; a concept critically important to nursing the older adult in acute care as well as in long-term care. Elders are vulnerable to physiologically induced delirium from infection, over-medication, and dehydration. The nursing home is an excellent setting to fine tune assessment skills, necessary to identifying the cause of confusion and appropriate nursing intervention. Interventions practiced in the nursing home take on a different dimension from interaction with younger patients in mental health settings. If a resident says, "My mother is next door," instead of the usual nursing interventions directed toward reality orientation, the student is taught to assist the elder in using the past to live more fully in the present, with responses such as "You miss your mother; tell me about her."

In Learning Management Skills

The nursing home setting provides opportunities for a wide variety of activities related to the management of patient care. Students can plan and assist in providing care for groups of residents. This can include giving medications and treatments to a group. Pre and postclinical conferences can focus on medication administration techniques and how they are adapted to respond to variables in the nursing home population.

Management of care includes use of the nursing process in assessing, planning, implementing, and evaluating care for a group of residents. Attendance at care conferences, revision of care plans, conferring with the physician or, where available, the nurse practitioner, helps students experience collaborative care. The latter also allows the student to see an advanced nursing role.

Other management experiences in the nursing home include supervision and evaluation of paraprofessionals. Time management, priority setting, and delegation of tasks can be carried out in the absence of the intense pressure often found in today's acute care setting. This may be the first time students have the opportunity to delegate and follow through.

Two major approaches to the structure of a management experience in the nursing home have been developed by project schools: placement of students with nursing home preceptors and forming student teams for practice of management skills. Shoreline College schedules a management experience in the nursing home for all second-year students, placing students one-on-one with staff nurses who have been prepared by college faculty to act as preceptors. One faculty person oversees a group of students and preceptors located in several nursing homes (see Appendix G). At Ohlone and Valencia Colleges, students elect to take a required management preceptorship in either the hospital or the nursing home. The few students who elect nursing home placement for management have typically identified the nursing home as the place they intent to work. In the second type of structure, students at Community College of Philadelphia are divided into teams that, as a group, care for a selected group of residents, and rotate through an assignment to perform team-leader functions for the group. Specified management objectives are met at that time; the team experience as a whole empowers the students and assists them in solidifying their professional role as team members.

BUT WHAT CONTENT IS *ESSENTIAL?*

At some point the faculty has to specify in detail the gerontological nursing content believed essential to the preparation of a graduate who is prepared to work in long-term care as well as acute hospital settings. A significant study by Kuehn (1991) provides the most useful (and valid) guide to date to identifying essential gerontological nursing content in the associate degree curriculum. Engaging two Delphi panels, one of associate degree nurse educators and another of nurses working in long-term care, Kuehn elicited agreement from these two groups on a core of essential content. Reprinted here in its entirety (Figure 4-1), Kuehn's list is inclusive of the topics selected by the six project faculty groups as they initiated curriculum change a few years earlier. Kuehn's findings offer useful discussion points for faculty, most particularly a comparison of the topics seen as important to practicing long-term care nurses but not educators, and vice versa.

Generating a list of important topics in gerontological nursing is not difficult. To the long list any interested faculty member could create without access to references, the table of contents of any gerontological nursing textbook will add even more topics. The challenge, of course, is in selecting what is important to teach, and in strategizing how to teach it in a limited time period. Each of the six faculty groups in the project schools discussed, negotiated, and argued about what to teach about gerontological nursing practice, and when and how to teach it. No two lists of topics ultimately selected in the project programs are alike; the consensus among all programs is in the strategies for clinical teaching in the nursing home, and in the new perspective across all courses in the curriculum. Kuehn's (1991) lists provide an invaluable resource to any faculty wishing to strengthen or add gerontological nursing content. We offer comments and suggestions about the following clusters of essential content, based on the experiences of our six faculty groups.

1. Demographics.
2. Attitudes toward aging.
3. Aging: A growth and development perspective.
4. Nursing process applied to the care of older patients.
5. Common health problems among elders.
6. The continuum of needs and services.
7. Ethical and legal issues.
8. Politics and public policy in health care for elders.

Demographics

The notion that the nature of nursing practice changes, reshaped as the needs of the population it serves change, is an important notion for students, and presentation of the data about the aging of U.S. society provides a dramatic example for discussion of that concept. Statistics regarding the incidence of acute and chronic illness and the use of health care services after age 65 are compelling when presented in combination with data regarding the projected numbers of people living to that age and older in the coming decades. The relative growth of the number of people who live to be 85 and older, a cohort heavily represented in nursing home populations, has particular impact on the health care system, and is of interest to students. Content on demographic trends and statistics might include life span data on males and females, effects of life experiences on age cohorts (for example, effects of the Great Depression and World War II on the current over-65 cohort), and other influences such as marital status, living conditions, geography, race, culture, education, and economics.

The demographic data is not hard to come by. Current nursing articles and textbooks frequently cite statistics. Official reports from the National Institute on Aging and the National Center for Health Statistics, as well as census data, are available for the asking. Local and regional information can be obtained from state and local offices of the so-called "Triple A's," Area Agencies on Aging (which go by one of a variety of names). These are federally mandated regional agencies assigned to coordinate a broad spectrum of services for the aged in local communities.

Attitudes toward Aging

Early nursing education research related to gerontological nursing studied student attitudes toward elderly patients and curriculum variables which might or might not affect those attitudes. Fostering interest in gerontological nursing practice among students and graduates remains a challenging task. After a comprehensive review of the literature on nursing student attitudes toward the elderly, Tagliareni (Tagliareni & Boring, 1988) concluded that there is no support for the practice of presenting one or more classes on attitude in preparation for clinical assignment to older patients. Instead, Tagliareni finds the order reversed: positive attitudes follow successful nursing interactions and interventions with older patients. The experience of faculty in the six project schools, all of whom were influenced by her findings, confirms her thesis. As a result, the emphasis is placed not on teaching "attitudes," per se, but rather on designing learning experiences which offer students a good chance of feeling competent, successful, and effective.

Figure 4-1
Essential Gerontological Nursing
Content for Associate Nurse Practice

Items Rated Essential by Both ADN Educators and LTC Nurses	Items Rated Essential by ADN Educators Only	Items Rated Essential by LTC Nurses Only
Commonly Encountered Health Problems	**Commonly Encountered Health Problems**	**Commonly Encountered Health Problems**
Abnormal bowel patterns	Anemia	AIDS†
Arthritis/collagen disease	Changes in immunity	Alzheimer's disease
Chronic brain syndrome	Deficits in health maintenance and prevention of illness/accidents	**Ethical Issues**
Cardiovascular	Drug dependency/addictions	Determining competency
Cerebrovascular	Drug/alcohol use	Quality of life issues
Delirium and confusion	Foot problems	Right to die/right to live
Dementias	Lack of activity and exercise factors which foster or impede	Right to refusal of treatment†
Depression	Malignancies	**Chronic Illness**
Diabetes mellitus	Polypharmacy	Patient-family interaction in long-term care†
Drug Interactions	Osteoporosis	**Growth and Development**
Falls	Reaction to relocation	Death and dying
Incontinence (bowel and bladder)	Specific drug classification	**Long-Term Care of Older Adults**
Infections	Suicide	Acute versus long-term care setting
Malnutrition/undernutrition	Surgery (untoward reactions)	Family reaction to long-term care
Medications	Syncope	**Nursing Process**
Pharmacokinetics related to older adults	**Ethical Issues**	Obtaining a health history
Pulmonary problems	Right to spiritual care	Appropriate documentation
Sensory deficits	Right to self-determination	Assessment categories
Skin lesions	**Chronic Illness**	Determination of ability to perform activities of daily living
Ethical Issues	Biological/physiological aspects	Determination of hearing acuity
Right to privacy	**Growth and Development**	Determination of visual acuity
Chronic Illness	Cognitive factors	Medications that improve/lower mental status
Accumulation of disabilities	Healthy older adult	Mental status assessment
Differences—acute and chronic Ilnesses	Learning characteristics	Use of functional assessment tools (eg, PULSES)
Individual responses	Psychology of older adult, theories	
Multiple chronic illnesses		
Psychosocial aspects		

Long-Term Care of Older Adults
Problems associated with activities of daily living in an institutional setting
Nursing Process
Obtaining a health history
Personal habits
Medical-surgical illness, immunizations, medications
Nutrition
Assessment categories
Functional assessment
Develop plan of action
Involve client/family caregivers in planning and establishing priorities
Provide for safety
Implement plan of care
Consistency of approach between caregivers
Individualize plan based on data/unique characteristics of the person
Evaluate care plan

Nursing Process
Interviewing techniques with older adults
Obtaining a health history
Fear/expectation of hospitalization
Health habits
Review of body systems
Social, economic factors
Stress reduction and methods of coping
Develop plan of action
Promote communication
Establish goals to maintain function and promote healthy lifestyle
Include teaching/learning
Rehabilitation
Evaluate care plan
Modify as appropriate based on reassessments
Maintain involvement of client and family in planning
Assessment categories
Identification of signs/symptoms of loss, grief, stress
Psychosocial assessment

Attitudes About Older Adults
Values clarification regarding aging

Role and Functions of the Nurse in Gerontology
Nursing impact on gerontology.

Politics of Aging
Impact on health-care personnel.

From: Kuehn, A. (1991). Essential gerontological content for the associate degree nursing curriculum: A national study. *Geriatric Nursing, 17,* 27. Reprinted with permission.

Project faculty have found that the first semester interactive experience with a well, older person living at home has been effective in its positive influence on student attitudes toward aging. Being with older adults in a variety of settings gives students a strong affinity and empathy for them, and may act as a strong motivator for choosing to care for older adults in nursing practice. In the nursing home itself, it is important to help the students set achievable goals and to structure learning experiences in relation to those goals.

Still, discussion of attitudes toward age in our culture is important. The negativism and ambivalence about aging that exists in our society are expressed in public policy decisions, in family decisions, and, clearly, in medical, nursing, and other health services. Attitudes toward aging should be exposed early in the curriculum and examined in each course. Classroom learning activities are available which are profoundly helpful to both students and faculty in identifying and responding to negative attitudes within themselves and in others. (See examples in Appendix D, and references to the simulation game, Into Aging, in Chapter 3). The first semester "well older adult" experience described earlier in this chapter (examples in Appendix A) have positively influenced student attitudes toward older people. Rather than lecture, it is important to design learning experiences which provide opportunities for students to reframe or rethink their ideas and beliefs about old age and older people.

Aging: A Growth and Development Perspective

A growth and development theme is part of virtually all associate degree curriculums, commonly introduced early in the program of study. Extending the nursing applications of developmental changes in human behavior to the understanding and care of the aged is a logical step for increasing gerontological content. With increasing frequency, growth and development courses include late-life ages and stages as well as the earlier decades. In some programs, faculties of anatomy and physiology, nutrition, psychology, and/or sociology have incorporated physical and sociocultural changes of aging in those courses. Systematic application of growth and development concepts throughout the curriculum is believed to be more effective than isolated lectures on the topic. Physical changes of aging can be highlighted and related to nursing management of particular categories of physiological dysfunction. Special handouts or fact sheets are helpful to students in integrating growth and development insights with the study of specific problems.

Psychological changes in aging are seen as an extension of the treatment of developmental tasks taught at various points in the program. Although Erikson (1963) dealt with the entire life cycle, faculty will find Peck's (1968) discussion of significant issues of later adulthood helpful. Students can fruitfully incorporate developmental tasks as described by both Erikson and Peck in care plans.

In our judgment, in growth and development discussions it is essential that students view aging not as a fixed chronological state, but as the next stage along a continuum of life events. The learning emphasis is on seeing the older adult as growing and developing, and focusing on the need of older adults to continuing to meet an array of developmental tasks. Aging is not limited to adjustment to decreasing capacities and acceptance of death as inevitable. Aging also involves striving to maintain a sense of autonomy and competence. Students can be asked to propose and carry out nursing interventions in all settings, but particularly in the hospital, that aid the older adult in trusting caregivers, maintaining autonomy and initiative, and fostering generativity and a positive sense of self as competent and interdependent. The focus is on the person, on the older adult's movement along a continuum of live events, a movement that signifies change and not necessarily decline. As Kuehn (1991) states:

The years, it's true, take your independence, your agility, your strength, and your friends. But they also give deeper meaning to work, to love, to sex, and to all the choices you've ever made.

Nursing Process Applied to the Care of Older Patients

The cluster of topics and learning activities selected by the faculty to teach the nursing process may vary from program to program, but nursing process is seen as central and basic in all ADN programs. Special considerations in the care of elders can be noted in relation to the steps of the nursing process. In assessment and history taking, physical examination techniques may need to be adapted for the older person because of sensory changes, cognitive limitations, decreased stamina, and others. Functional and cognitive assessments of the elderly patient are as important of physical assessment, and the nursing home clinical provides excellent opportunities for developing these skills. (See Appendix E for sample clinical activities.)

Setting goals or establishing plans is important to the care of older adults in all settings. Along with responding to the direction specified by the medical plan of care, there is the opportunity to create a comprehensive nursing perspective by incorporating goals related to health promotion, rehabilitation, maintenance of optimal functional ability, or the support of decline.

Nursing interventions frequently need to be adapted to age-related variables in the elderly, as indeed they are adapted for other age groups, particularly children. In selecting and adapting a particular intervention, the student is coached to think about evaluation, and to propose how it will be accomplished in cognizance of the older adult's life style, rituals and routines, and available supports. The sharp reduction in the duration of a hospital stay over the past decade has eroded the opportunities for students to observe outcomes of nursing care and evaluate the effectiveness of plans and interventions. The nursing home, on the other hand, provides time for reflection and evaluation that is, for students, effective and highly satisfying.

Common Health Problems Among Elders

In response to a recent survey of associate degree nursing programs by Hanson (in press) requesting information about gerontologic nursing content in the curriculum, respondents had more difficulty identifying what was allocated to the subtopic "common health problems" than any other. The survey yielded reasonably precise data regarding instruction about demographics, attitudes toward aging, growth and development, and legal and ethical issues, but responses to questions about the teaching of nursing responses to common health problems associated with aging was, in the words of the researcher, "fuzzy." The concern raised by this finding is that where faculty are hard-pressed to identify what is taught in a given content area, students are undoubtedly left with a similarly vague picture of that topic. Integrating age-related considerations throughout the curriculum can be effective, but unless it is systematically planned and accounted for, it is all too frequently "lost." We take the position that whatever design is selected by faculty for including gerontologic nursing, there needs to be distinct visibility and emphasis on the special problems of the frail elderly in institutional long term care settings, namely:

Safety.
Nutrition and dentition.

Mental health care.
Mobility.
Preventing infection.
Managing incontinence.
Integumentary integrity.
Fluid and electrolyte balance.
Drug use and abuse.

Safety, mobility, and managing incontinence are suited to topics universally included in fundamentals instruction. Nutrition, dentition, and mental health are priorities of care for the frail elderly in long-term care. Although nutrition is commonly a subject in the first-year curriculum, assigning students to a nutrition and diet assessment during a second-year nursing home clinical helps to emphasize the importance of this aspect of patient management in the elderly population. In community colleges with dental hygiene programs, the significance of dentition to the well-being of older adults, and the range of interventions, can be taught to nursing students by dental hygiene faculty, as it is at Shoreline. Mental health care, including problems associated with depression, confusion, and relocation stress can be introduced and developed in second level courses in acute care as well as long-term settings.

Infections (URI and UTI) and fluids and electrolyte problems in elders can be comfortably integrated into other courses dealing with adult patients, and presented as an age-related variable. (See Appendix B for examples of student Fact Sheets on this topic.)

We have found it useful to allocate up to two hours of lecture time to emphasize the very important topic of drug use and misuse in treatment of the elderly. It is critical that the issues and standards regarding pharmacology and polypharmacy be reinforced in the clinical component of the program. Students benefit from a focused assignment about polypharmacy. (See example in Appendix F.)

The Continuum of Needs and Services

A graduate of one of the project programs, employed in a nursing home and invited back to the college to participate in a critique of her student experience in gerontological nursing, admonished the faculty to include more experience with discharge planning of hospitalized patients "since most of them are 85 and their choices are so complex." Nurse educators believe that teaching for continuity of care is important, but typically provide few learning experiences other than direct care to acutely ill patients.

Project programs have assigned students to visit senior citizen centers, housing complexes for seniors, adult day care services, and homes. A community service panel of representatives from local agencies has been included in a class schedule.

Kuehn's (1991) study of essential gerontological content for the associate degree curriculum leads her to observe that "a consistent theme . . . is acknowledgment of a role for the ADN outside the acute and long-term care settings" (p. 25). She identifies an ADN community role, different than and complementary to the baccalaureate or advanced practitioner role, as one that includes discharge planning of hospitalized patients and practicing in clinics and home health agencies (p. 25).

Ethical and Legal Issues

Since the inception of the Partnership project, there have been a number of striking insights for faculty who have been teaching the nursing home, but none more dramatic than a new perspective on the ethical and legal issues and dilemmas related to health care for older people. Before their intensive association with the nursing home, project faculty were probably not unlike the ADN educators who, in responding to Kuehn's (1991) study, indicated that essential content within ethical issues included privacy, spiritual care, and self-determination. Kuehn's long-term care practicing nurse respondents, however, rated the following as essential:

Determining competency.
Quality of life issues.
Right to die/right to live.
Right to refusal of treatment.
(see Figure 4-1)

Without question, ethical issues have become much more complex in acute care settings as well, and nursing (and related) literature provides new help for faculty trying to master the critical points in this mushrooming subject area (see especially Davis & Aroskar, 1991; Kane & Caplan, 1990). Major topics which we believe must be considered essential in the nursing curriculum today will be discussed briefly, recognizing that any faculty member new to this subject will need to seek more explanatory and complete sources.

The *Patients Self-Determination Act*, part of OBRA 1990 and in effect since October 1, 1991, requires every acute care hospital, nursing home, home care agency, and HMO receiving Medicare and Medicaid funds to establish and share with each patient on admission policies and procedures regarding patient rights, the right to refuse treatment, and advanced directives.

An *Advanced Directive* is any valid set of instructions such as a "living will" or durable power of attorney that the individual executes while competent.

Assessing for Competency or for Decision-Making is a challenge to health care providers. Students can learn that competency is not an all or nothing state; it is relative in relation to the decision to be made. A person may lack competence for financial decisions, but retain competency for decisions regarding care and treatment.

Benefits and Burdens are increasingly cited in decisions about whether or not to follow a particular course of treatment. Weighing whether the benefits projected from the treatment are greater than the burdens the treatment effects will impose is seen as the most rational way to make decisions. Still, the relative weight of each is wholly personal, and the role of the nurse is not to impose but to assist.

The *Right to Refuse Treatment*, which assumes *informed consent*, has weighty implications for nursing action. There is an obligation to provide the patient with all the information needed to make an informed decision, yet not influence that decision. The nurse now has increased responsibility for the consequences of any action taken that is contrary to the patient's wishes. A patient's desire for *autonomy*, however, is closely tied to cultural, educational, and ethnic characteristics, and the nurse must make individual assessments. (See examples of learning activities in Appendix H).

Withholding and withdrawing nutrition and hydration is an issue of the right to refuse treatment, and a major dilemma in the nursing home.

Ethics committees, in existence in medical centers for some time, are now being formed by many long-term care facilities to help resolve issues such as nutrition and hydration, do-not-resuscitate orders, and other troubling dilemmas. An excellent video, entitled "Ethics Committees: Allies in Long-Term Care,'" is available from American Association of Retired Persons (AARP) for sale or loan; we urge its inclusion in your classroom activities. A companion booklet lists other resources (AARP, 1990).

Politics and Public Policy

Health care services for older citizens periodically have fostered a debate and rhetoric in the political arena; the visibility and sometime contentiousness of difficult issues will only increase with the continued growth in the size of the older population. Students benefit from gaining insight into the relationships between public policy positions and nursing home resources and services.

Both the National League for Nursing and the American Nurses' Association are active in the public policy arena as advocates for health care for the elderly. Both enunciate strong positions through membership structures (in NLN, the Board of Governor's Long-Term Care Committee, and, in ANA, the Council on Gerontological Nursing) and maintain active contacts with elected officials and federal agency staff members. Current positions and activities of the organizations can be found in *Nursing & Health Care* and *The American Nurse,* or requests for material can be directed to the staff of either organization. Students should be made aware of major organizational initiatives, and given an opportunity to discuss them. Public policy issues that provoke student discussion include government allocation of support for long-term care insurance, rationing of care, and the politics of fueling intergenerational competition for government funds (should we spend tax dollars on the last weeks and months of life, or to help children?).

IN SUMMARY—SOME DOs AND DON'Ts

1. Don't make the change to add gerontology to the curriculum a "big deal" for students or faculty.
2. Do use resources and curriculum content at hand—apply basic concepts purposefully to the elderly.
3. Do provide small group time to discuss attitudes and perceptions.
4. Do have fun while fostering positive attitudes through creative games and classroom exercises.
5. Do provide a student experience with well older adults.
6. Do provide a second year nursing home clinical experience for each student.
7. Don't think that "we" are doing "them" a favor.
8. Don't try to make everyone "like" the nursing home.
9. Do develop your own support group.
10. Do bring to center stage the faculty who have positive interests in gerontological nursing and the nursing home.

11. Do encourage faculty to take courses, workshops, and the gerontology certification exam.
12. Do allow time for change; it doesn't happen overnight.
13. Do think about and plan for the nursing home experience based on what competencies students will learn best.
14. Do design clinical experiences in the nursing home carefully.
15. Do realize there is a great deal to learn about the elderly in the nursing home.
16. Do keep gerontological nursing concepts as a thread in the curriculum.
17. Do give careful thought to a capstone, second year, separate course focusing on gerontological nursing and institutional long-term care.
18. Do keep looking for the right text in gerontological nursing.
19. Do look for fundamentals and med-surg texts that make specific applications to geriatric patients.
20. Do add ideas about demographic trends, nursing responsibility to serve the elderly, and the goal of preparing graduates who are prepared to work in both acute and long-term care to your framework or curriculum narrative.
21. Don't think you have gerontology in the curriculum just because most of the patients your students care for in the hospital are over 65.
22. Do recruit faculty to work with and support you who are leaders, who like change, or who have power positions. They may not be the ones who know the most about gerontology.
23. Do select nursing homes where staff feels connected to the mission of the facility.
24. Don't make long-term care seem less than acute care.
25. Do help students differentiate between "cure" and "care" practices.
26. Do take time to learn the nursing home, and try to understand it.
27. Do start—just do it!

REFERENCES

American Association of Colleges of Nursing. (1986). *Essentials of college and university education for professional nursing.* Washington, DC: Author.

American Nurses Association (1987). *Standards and scope of gerontological nursing practice.* Kansas City, MO: ANA

Davis, A.J. & Aroskar, M.A. (1991). *Ethical dilemmas and nursing practice.* Norwalk, CT: Appleton & Lange.

Erikson, E. (1963). *Childhood and society.* New York: Norton.

Hanson, H. (in press). *Newslink.* (Available from Community College-Nursing Home Partnership, Community College of Philadelphia, 1700 Spring Garden Street, Philadelphia, PA 19130).

Kane, R., & Caplan, A. (Eds.) (1990). *Everyday ethics: Resolving dilemmas in nursing home life.* New York: Springer.

Kuehn, A. (1991). Essential gerontological content for the associate degree nursing curriculum: A national study. *Geriatric Nursing, 17,* 20–27.

National League for Nursing (1989). Resolutions voted on at closing business meeting. *Nursing & Health Care, 10,* 385.

National League for Nursing (1988). *Strategies for long-term care.* New York: The League.

Peck, R.C. (1968). Psychological developments in the second half of life. In Neugarten, B., (Ed.), *Middle age and aging.* Chicago: University of Chicago Press.

Tagliareni, E., & Boring, G. (1988). Faculty, student, caregiver attitudes toward the aged. In *Associate degree nursing and the nursing home.* New York: National League for Nursing, 99–112.

5

Developing and Maintaining the Learning Environment

Mary Ann Anderson
Gail M. Cobe

INTRODUCTION

Since the inception of the Community College-Nursing Home Partnership, project faculty have become increasingly enthusiastic about the significance of the nursing home as a clinical teaching site. The nursing home is a unique environment, a setting where nursing judgments are paramount and where a nursing model of care can be made real and explored by students. It is a setting where collaborative relationships are essential to individualization of care and where students have the opportunity to learn through close clinical collaboration with staff, with faculty, and with each other. A project faculty member has observed that the most fundamental teaching and learning benefit from the nursing home is that it is *not* the hospital. Her observation is a comment on the educational richness of the nursing home, but it also points to the fact that faculty need to teach differently than they do in the hospital.

In this chapter, we will discuss the faculty member's initial and continuing contacts and relationships in clinical education in the nursing home.

While there have been differences among the nursing homes used for
student placement in the six project sites, and different faculty experiences, there also are strong commonalities in the experience that allow
us to generalize and share the recommended steps and strategies that
follow.

GETTING STARTED

Chapter 3 describes activities to enhance the nursing faculty's knowledge and understanding of long-term care nursing; Chapter 4 notes the
importance of total faculty involvement in decisions about essential content and the allocation of clinical and classroom time to long-term care
and the nursing home. Once these decisions are made, the designation
of one or more members of the clinical teaching faculty to conduct the
clinical classes in the nursing home is of considerable consequence. A
thoughtful and systematic approach to the first phase of a new relationship
between the nursing program and nursing home is important to its long-
range success.

Whether the designation of faculty members to teach in the nursing
home is the outcome of self-selection or administrative assignment, it is
important for a program adding substantive new educational experiences
for students in the nursing home to entrust the initiation and development
of the new experience to instructors who, in addition to having a working
knowledge of gerontological nursing, hold the respect and regard of others
on the faculty. The stereotypes, negative opinions, and pessimism held
by many nurse educators toward nursing homes create doubt about the
potential success of clinical affiliation. To the extent possible, the participation of faculty seen as leaders will counter the influence of such deleterious factors. A strong faculty member serves as a role model not only for
students and nursing home staff, but for faculty as well.

Faculty who have expressed an interest in exploring new teaching
methodologies and in re-examining teacher–student–nursing staff relationships in the clinical setting also are good candidates for teaching in
the nursing home. As Chapter 6 will describe, we have found new
teaching roles and behaviors emerging as faculty have adjusted to the
nursing home setting.

Advice can be directed to the individual faculty members who are
ultimately assigned to the nursing home clinical. Project faculty learned
the value of developing a network of long-term care nurses who become

an important resource and source of support. Directors of nursing (DON) and directors of staff development (DSD) from affiliating nursing homes formed the core of the network. In some settings, new relationships developed with graduate faculty in local university gerontological nursing programs or the nearest federally funded Geriatric Education Center (GEC). Most localities have an organization of long-term care nurses, under the sponsorship of the American Health Care Association (the trade association for proprietary nursing homes), or as a unit of the state nurses association. The network, and participation in long-term care nursing organizational activity, gives the faculty member the opportunity to learn the culture and language of institutional long-term care nursing, and to identify potential resources both for students and faculty.

When the faculty member has not previously worked in a nursing home, time should be arranged to spend several days—we recommend from five to ten—in the facility. It is important to spend time with all levels of staffs, and direct-service departments such as physical therapy and dietary. It is significant to everyone in a facility to see a positive relationship established with the director of nursing and the staff developer. Ample time needs to be allotted to working with the nursing assistants, building rapport with them, observing the relationship that exists between the nursing assistant and the resident, and learning the unstated yet important values and beliefs that guide the nursing assistant's practice. Project faculty have reported that an important aspect of getting ready is identifying a supportive person in the nursing home who will serve as mentor, answer questions, and point out the idiosyncracies of the facility. In effect, then, the faculty member who enters a nursing home to foster an effective instructional environment requires:

- An interest and intent to continue advancing his or her knowledge in gerontological nursing.
- A network and support system of gerontological nurses who work in nursing homes to use as a source of reference.
- The ability to model nursing behaviors to students in the nursing home.
- Willingness to explore a new teaching role and teaching strategies in the new setting.

COLLABORATIVE PLANNING FOR A LEARNING ENVIRONMENT

The importance of early thoughtful planning and discussion with the director of nursing cannot be overemphasized. Through (and with) the director, the faculty member should meet and talk with the facility administrator as well, gaining endorsement of the educational affiliation, and describing the methods of clinical nursing education.

At this meeting, the contract to provide clinical placements and other procedural matters may be discussed. Point out the positive outcomes for both parties of a successful affiliation. Share the findings of a study in which directors of nursing homes reported that the major benefits of an education affiliation are:

- *Increased educational opportunities for nursing home staff.*
- *Enhanced staff image of nurses in long-term care.*
- *Positive influence of students on nursing home staff.*
- *Broadened relationships with the college and the community. (Carignan, 1989)*

Plan to leave a small amount of carefully selected additional reading for the nursing home administrator, with copies for the DON. Consider developing a one- to two-page summary of the curriculum rather than leaving course descriptions or syllabi. A short, particularly relevant article (or a few pages photocopied from this book) might be of interest to add to the administrator's understanding of educational purposes and methods in nursing. It is important to leave only a few pages, and to point out the salient features of the material you are providing.

Meetings with the DON, RNs, and LPNs (LVNs) should allow time for discussion of purposes and expectations each holds for the affiliation. Student objectives need to be clearly presented with time for examples and questions. Review the clinical evaluation tool, clarifying meanings, and invite the facility staff to share responsibility for helping the students achieve stated clinical objectives.

Provide support and coaching for the director of nursing in anticipation of questions from idealistic students challenging standards, procedures, and motivation in the nursing home. Point out to students the importance of their exchanges with the director, and convey your intention to work with the director in responding to student concerns, both realistic and unrealistic.

It is as important for the faculty member in the nursing home to establish close collaborative relationships with nursing assistants. Their knowledge of residents becomes an important resource to faculty and students; their support of educational activities is essential to students realizing their objectives. It is important that nursing assistants understand your educational plans and strategies, and know the objectives the students are expected to meet. In addition to formal or semi-formal initial meetings, the instructor should talk with nursing home staff on a weekly basis to specify the clinical objectives or learning focus for the week. This assists the staff in planning their own care, and prepares them for the type of questions students will be asking. For example, if the student focus is on cognitive assessment, students will, in addition to interacting with assigned patients, ask questions of the staff regarding the resident's level of confusion or medical history.

Similarly, the staff nurses and director of nursing are experts in that setting, and it is important that the faculty and students recognize and what act on that fact. Like the hospital nurse, the long-term care nurse may wonder if he or she measures up in the eyes of the academic or the more up-to-date student, and be less than forthcoming with what he or she knows about nursing practice. The faculty member can provide opportunities for nursing staff to share their expertise with students. Here, the primary emphasis is to provide students with opportunities to learn how nurses in the long-term care institutional setting make decisions and what factors influence those decisions. In one example, the resident being cared for by a student suffered a Transient Ischemic Attack (TIA). The student's first response was to recommend laboratory work and removal to a hospital for emergency care. The director of nursing, with whom the student discussed the resident's condition, told her that this was not an unusual episode, and that the dizziness went away if the resident lay in bed under a warm blanket with head elevated. The student did that, and, after a nap, the resident awoke, dizziness gone, and expressed gratitude to the student for "saving my life." Nursing decisions in the nursing home are often significantly different than in the hospital, and students sometimes see them as uncaring or incompetent; the participation of the director of nursing and licensed staff is needed to assist students in gaining a different perspective.

The essential factors in a successful relationship between an ADN program and a nursing home are:

- *Mutual respect and understanding.*
- *A commitment to high quality education for students.*
- *A commitment to high quality service to clients.*
- *A collaborative approach to managing the affiliation. (Mengel, Simson, Sherman, & Waters, 1991)*

These authors also noted that even where the nursing home is an active and interested partner, the college assumes the larger responsibility for maintaining the partnership, simply because it has more resources and experience with academic affiliations.

A number of collaborative activities developed between project schools and partner nursing homes which served to strengthen working relationships and improve the learning environment for students include:

- Short, often informal, but sometimes tightly structured, inservice given by faculty for nursing home staff. This is accomplished at times by faculty reasoning aloud in the presence of staff members.

- An invitation to the director of nursing or facility administrator to serve on the nursing program advisory board.

- An invitation to the faculty member or nursing program director to serve on the nursing home board or an advisory committee.

- Group meetings organized (where none exist) for local area directors of nursing and/or staff developers. Faculty can facilitate early sessions, enabling them to become support groups.

- Surplus copies of textbooks and other learning materials may be donated by faculty to nursing homes with limited budgets.

- A lending library of books, videos, and other learning materials may be established for nursing homes.

- Active participation of the director of nursing and other staff in orienting students to the facility. Nursing assistants especially like to be included in orientation, since they know the daily routine and can speak to each resident as an individual.

- Class presentation by a panel of local area directors of nursing on issues, trends, and opportunities in long-term care, or presentations by a director of nursing and other staff in classes about long-term care for the frail elderly.

- Invitation to the director of nursing and administrator, along with acute care representatives, to attend faculty retreats or curriculum workshops.

- Invitation to director of nursing and other nursing home RNs to join faculty attending local or regional conferences and meetings.

- Invitation to staff developers to previews of educational videos and textbook evaluation discussions.

ENHANCING THE LEARNING ENVIRONMENT BY CONTRIBUTING TO STAFF DEVELOPMENT

The collaborative activities listed above include several that represent faculty efforts to share knowledge with the nursing home staff. Since 75 to 90 percent of nursing home employees are nursing assistants, and since most of the direct care is given by this group, the potential and the reward for using opportunities to contribute to their knowledge and skill is great. A solid mutually respectful relationship is a basic requirement. Project faculty have initiated or been asked to present demonstration and discussion sessions on wide-ranging topics: observing for skin changes, signs of infection, communicating with an angry resident, evaluating cognitive function (simplified), and patient rights, to name a few. Nursing assistants are invited to attend post-conferences when residents under their care are discussed, both contributing to and learning from the discussion. They are welcomed at bedside demonstrations and discussions between faculty and student. Their knowledge of the resident is considered, and their advice sought regarding interventions that require participation or follow-up on their part. Faculty and students provide feedback to the nursing assistants about suggestions, opinions, and concerns they express, thereby encouraging continued open communication.

PROBLEMS, REAL AND IMAGINED

From the time when a project proposal was first submitted to the W.K. Kellogg Foundation, we expected that a new clinical affiliation with a nursing home would be accompanied by a set of activities initiated by faculty and designed to enlarge the skills and abilities of the nursing home staff. What was unexpected was the extent of employee turnover in the nursing home, at all levels of staff. There are wide variations: a not-for-profit facility with a close-knit staff and strong institutional identity and traditions or a facility serving a small rural community may have very low turnover; another type of nursing home in another place may have 100 percent turnover in a year's time. Our initial dismay has been tempered by the observation over time that while nursing home employees, nurses, and their assistants alike may leave a given nursing home, they more often than not take a position at another within the same community. As educators with a compelling interest in promoting clinical education in the nursing home, we have acknowledged that efforts to develop supportive learning environments for students must be directed at the individuals who are employed in them rather than at the nursing home as an institution. In effect, this means that each time an instructor takes a new group of students to a nursing home, there is a need to evaluate staff changes and plan accordingly.

If staff changes have been greater than at first expected by project faculty, a second concern about the nursing home environment has been less problematic than common wisdom among nurse educators predicts. The nursing home environment is generally held to be a *poor* learning environment, attributable to a substandard quality of care and a lack of good role models for students. Our experiences of several years convince us that apart from any judgment on care standards and performance abilities, which vary as they do in all health delivery systems, the nursing home is not in fact a *poor* learning environment, but indeed *rich.* Its richness lies in its ability to provide students with opportunity to explore a nursing model of care delivery, and to focus nursing interventions on the restoration of functional ability and enhancement of the quality of life. Chapter 6 will describe, in detail, learning activities in the nursing home designed to highlight this perspective and provide students with deeply affecting, wholly positive learning experiences.

CONCLUSION

Success in the development of the learning environment in the nursing home lives in its organization and thoughtfulness. This chapter has outlined approaches that strengthen the relationship and contribute to the development of the nursing home staff as the central factor in the learning environment. We have not discussed conference rooms, lockers, or lunch facilities, nor have we found them important to the quality of student experience. We have emphasized the importance of a carefully planned beginning affiliation, and the need for continuing evaluation of staff as well as students as they interact in activities relevant to the educational program. Approaches to educating nursing students to function in specialized care of elderly in long-term care settings are not only new to most faculty members, but are still evolving in educational practice. Finally, we offer the following list of suggested readings for understanding the nature of the nursing home environment. Students as well as faculty may find these books and articles helpful.

SUGGESTED READINGS

Bennett, C. (1980). *Nursing home life: What it is and what it could be.* New York: The Tiresias Press.

The author entered a nursing home masquerading as a patient. He describes his experiences in conversational style, with funny but serious cartoons. This inexpensive paperback provides a good picture of nursing home life.

McNamara, R. M. (1986). Working in a long-term care facility: How does it compare with working in a hospital? *Nursing 86 12,* 53.

Gives a clear and easy-to-read comparison between the two work worlds from the nurse's perspective. This article is particularly good for students to understand the nursing home environment.

O'Brien, M. E. (1989). *Anatomy of a nursing home: A new view of resident life.* Owings Mill, MD: National Health.

Based on a research project supported by Robert Wood Johnson Foundation and Catholic University. An easy-to-read narrative takes the reader on a tour of the residents, world, discussing religion, death, family support, relationships, stresses, ethics, and more. Good references are provided.

Retsinas, J. (1986). *It's OK mom: The nursing home from a sociological perspective.* New York: The Tiresias Press.

This short, inexpensive, paperback is written in popular language, and gives an accurate description of nursing home life. It clearly shows and explains the reasons for the differences in the environments of acute and long-term care settings. The author both compliments and criticizes nursing homes.

REFERENCES

Carignan, A. (1990). Partnership impact on nursing home care. Unpublished. In M. A. Anderson (Ed.), Collaborative relationships: A key to success. *NEWSLINK,* Spring issue. (Available from Community College-Nursing Home Partnership, Community College of Philadelphia, 1700 Spring Garden Street, Philadelphia, PA 19130).

Mengel, A., Simpson, S., Sherman, S., & Waters, V. (1990). Essential factors in a community college-nursing home partnership. *Gerontological Nursing, 16,* 26–31.

6

What and How of
Student Learning Activities

Elaine Tagliareni

SARAH'S STORY

Sarah stood by the elevator in the nursing home waiting for her clinical instructor to arrive. Sarah greeted her saying, "It's the third week of this rotation and I'm getting nowhere with Anna. All she ever says is, 'Do I live here? Is this my room? Where is my apartment?' I am so discouraged."

Sarah and her instructor walked off to talk with Anna. Together they conducted a thorough assessment and brainstormed about creative approaches to help Anna become more involved in daily activities at the nursing home. While conducting the interview, Sarah began to realize that Anna was less cognitively impaired than she had suspected at first and suggested that maybe Anna could manage quiet group events. As luck would have it, that day in the nursing home, the group was playing trivial pursuit. As Sarah and Anna entered the dayroom, the group leader called out, "Oh, here is Sarah! What is the longest river in the United States?" Sarah answered immediately, "Why it's the Mississippi, isn't it?" Standing next to her, Anna quietly murmured, "No, dear; it's the Missouri." At that moment, Sarah saw Anna differently.

65

*The following week, Sarah arrived to find that Anna had been trans-
ferred to the coronary unit of a local acute care hospital. Sarah called the
CCU nurse and asked about Anna. The nurse told Sarah all about
Anna's blood levels, oxygen saturation, and cardiac status. Sarah asked
again, "But how is Anna?" The CCU nurse said, "How would I know?
All she ever says is, 'Do I live here? Is this my room? Where is my
apartment?' " As she ended the conversation, Sarah said to the CCU
nurse, "You would be surprised how much Anna really knows."*

*Later that day, Sarah talked with her instructor. She had been thinking
all day about her conversation with the CCU nurse. "I now know what
I wanted to say to that CCU nurse. Do you know the longest river in the
United States? Anna does. I wanted to say to that nurse, Go ahead and
ask her; it will make all the difference; I know it did for me."*

Sarah is right. Understanding the older adult, appreciating the value
of maintenance of functional ability, recognizing the uniqueness of the
individual in today's technologically complex modern health care system
are all critical learning activities of a new curriculum which actively
integrates gerontological concepts. Nurses today must be competent caregivers with older adults. The demographics and the changing picture
of disease, where individuals with chronic illness and multiple system
involvement are the primary seekers of health care in a variety of settings,
compel nurse educators to shift from a totally acute care, hospital-based
curriculum. Sarah's story illustrates, too, the dilemma experienced by
nurses and nursing students today: how to be a caring, humanistic professional with holistic philosophy in a system that is medically oriented,
where services are fragmented, where individuals, like Anna, are often
overlooked and dehumanized. In this chapter, then, I will discuss specific
learning activities and methodologies that help students understand the
dilemma and that help students see themselves as caring, humanistic
professionals through experiences with older adults, in both acute and
long-term care settings.

Three interrelated assumptions are important here:

1. Students today must be competent caregivers with older adults in
   general and the frail older adult in particular. This means that they
   must know the older adult as an individual, appreciate the impact
   of the aging process and environmental factors on the delivery
   of nursing care to older adults, and actively pursue rehabilitation
   potentials despite the presence of functional and cognitive impair-

ment and chronic illness. The nursing home provides a rich environment to focus on these competencies.

2. Students must experience nursing in a setting where the focus is on
   rehabilitation, maintenance of functional ability, and promotion of
   quality of life. Students must be provided an opportunity to create
   therapeutic environments away from the tubes and the machines of
   the acute care system. A second level, well-designed nursing home
   experience provides that exposure. When students experience the
   sense of empowerment that comes from assisting ill persons to
   improve their quality of life, without regard for their cure potential,
   they begin to understand the caring ethic of nursing. Students today
   practice nursing in a "world seized by technology" (Boyd, 1988). A
   key curriculum focus is to assist students to transfer learning from
   the nursing home to the acute care setting and to recognize the
   value of maintenance and rehabilitation in both settings. A curriculum that is solely acute care and hospital focused is not adequate to
   accomplish this mandate.

3. When teaching methods foster a sense of empowerment with older
   adults in both care and cure settings, students will develop positive
   attitudes toward older adults. Attitudes change as students develop
   specific knowledge and skills to be effective caregivers with frail
   older adults, when they realize that by embracing rehabilitation
   potentials and valuing maintenance of function they can make a
   difference in their lives. Attitudes follow effectiveness; they do not
   precede it.

These three assumptions can be considered general goals for a curriculum that seeks to fully integrate gerontology. They are criteria for selecting
and devising learning experiences and for guiding teacher–student interactions. They give faculty a direction that becomes the rubric under which
a wide range of learning experiences and content can fall, depending on
each school's organizing framework (Bevis & Watson, 1989). In this
chapter, I will describe learning activities that have been utilized in
project schools to address these general assumptions.

MOVING TOWARD COMPETENT PRACTICE WITH OLDER ADULTS: PROVIDING GUIDEPOSTS

When faculty begin to think about gerontological integration they
often ask, "where do I begin?" It's a tough question if gerontological

integration is conceptualized as additional content to add to an already overextended curriculum; it's an exciting question when integration is envisioned as assisting students to know older adults as individuals in a variety of settings and to be empowered caregivers. When the latter perspective guides curriculum design, a new focus on existing content falls into place and *more* content is not added.

Changing Focus

Most nursing programs integrate the history of nursing early in the program. As faculty at one project school began the process of gerontological integration, they redesigned this learning experience in the introductory nursing course. Nursing was presented as a profession that has consistently altered its course to respond positively to changes in society (wars, immigration, the industrial revolution, and so on). Students were asked to think about changes in contemporary society that impact on the delivery of health care. This led to a lively discussion of the changing demographics, the increased numbers of old-old who require long-term care both at home and in nursing homes, and the high acuity and rapid turnover of patients in hospitals. Faculty highlighted not only the implications for nursing practice, but helped the student to understand that precisely because of these changes, their learning experiences for the next four semesters would have a heavy emphasis on aging and nursing care of older adults. They would be provided with clinical experiences in both acute and long-term care settings in order to appreciate the different types of settings where nursing is practiced today. What fascinated the faculty member conducting the seminar was how quickly the students identified current trends and how they nodded their heads in agreement when the curriculum was explained. The faculty member may have needed convincing that a curriculum which emphasizes nursing care of the older adult was acceptable; for the student it seemed a logical and natural focus!

Socialization to the nursing role is another theme that is commonly developed in the introductory nursing course. This content often focuses on identification of associate degree nursing (ADN) competencies and introduces different levels of nursing education and types of nursing practice—an overview of the profession. In a curriculum with gerontological integration and a second level nursing home experience, students might be asked to think about the profession of nursing in relation to medical practice. Do the disciplines overlap? How? If follow through on the medical care plan is part of nursing practice, what do the other parts look like? Here students might be introduced to the concepts of maintenance of functional ability, rehabilitation potentials, and nursing's commitment to provide support in grief and dying. The concept that nursing always has assisted ill persons without regard for their cure potential is emphasized. Then these ideas are related to the specific educational outcomes of the AD nurse; the student learns the basic concepts of the role of the AD nurse but with a focus that assists the student to define nursing as *more* than curative in scope. Students begin to articulate this perspective early in their nursing career. In a log written on the second week of clinical, after providing complete care for the first time, a fundamentals student wrote:

> *Just as we were ready to leave, lunch arrived and we prepared Ms. K.'s tray for her to eat. She looked at the tray, sighed and turned away.*
>
> *So my partner went to give report and I stayed and fed her as much as she wanted, urging her to eat a little more. This one act made me feel competent. Nursing is not strictly technical, medical care; it's human, one-to-one being there for each other.*
>
> S. J. F., CCP student

Another student in fundamentals speaks to the paradox of humanism amidst technology, which she has been encouraged to ponder:

> *I see nursing as being a mediator between the cut and dry, black and white, technical medical field, and the very gray area of just being human with patients.*
>
> D. Z., CCP student

Integration of Content About Aging

Faculty often ask: Is aging content best taught in a block with concomitant experience in long-term care or should it be integrated? The answer again relates to the focus of the curriculum. If faculty work from the assumption that students today must be effective caregivers with older adults and that older adults constitute the largest segment of patients in acute and long-term care, then the older adult becomes the paradigm case to teach fundamental concepts about nursing. Basic concepts about nursing and nursing practice are given a new focus. For example, as faculty introduce the basic physiological concepts of oxygenation and circulation in a curriculum seeking to integrate gerontology, students would be informed about norms for the older adult as well as standard norms. Both sets of criteria for assessment of physiological status are normal and adaptive. In project schools, faculty have developed "fact sheets" describing aging norms with significant implications for nursing care which students utilize for physical assessments and for writing care plans. As the curriculum progresses and individual common health problems are discussed, students learn about unique presentations in the older adult. Sample fact sheets are provided in Appendix B.

Project faculty also have introduced basic concepts of therapeutic communication using the older adult as the "norm." Students are introduced to major stressors and losses affecting the older adult and to unique communication techniques that encourage expression of feelings, for example, reminiscence. Films and videotapes are shown to illustrate effective communication with older adults. Students utilize this information as a foundation for more advanced content in therapeutic communication. After all, most fundamentals students clearly spend the greater majority of their clinical time with older adults. By assisting the student to communicate effectively with the first group of patients they care for clinically, students are given the basic tools to be competent practitioners. This is the beginning of empowerment.

One very important theme that must run parallel to integration of physiological and psychosocial aging content is the changing character of contemporary illness. Epidemiologists describe today's disease picture as the age of degeneration disease, where health professionals treat the acute exacerbations of chronic illness (but not the chronic illness itself) and individuals with chronic illness survive. Students today rarely meet a patient with one acute illness. Nursing practice involves care of individuals with multiple system involvement, who experience an acute exacerbation of one common health problem, with chronic conditions remaining and requiring nursing care. We have found it helpful to provide students with experiences, both in the classroom and in clinical, to study the older adult in this context and to recognize that curative care has its limits. Especially with the frail older adult, students learn to see the individual, to recognize that even when cure is not possible rehabilitation, increased performance, and maintenance of function usually is. Unless students embrace this idea, we have not been successful in integrating gerontological nursing content by providing them with opportunities to to ponder this perspective in the second level nursing home clinical experience.

The Well Elderly Experience

When asked: "Where do I begin gerontological integration?", project faculty often suggest the well elderly experience. As described in Chapter 4, project faculty have incorporated community-based well elderly experiences into introductory nursing courses (see Appendix A). Students gain a broader perspective on the aging process, and begin to appreciate the older adult's need to maintain previous life tasks that have been successfully achieved, and to acknowledge the older adult's strength and wisdom. These experiences serve as additional guideposts to ground students in knowledge of normal aging before caring for the older adult in both acute and long-term settings. But faculty cannot assume that the well elderly experience in the community will, by itself, prepare students for work with elderly in institutional settings. Faculty must actively assist students to transfer learning gleamed from the well elder to the frail older adult. Students need guidance to make the leap from reminiscing with an older, active, intact adult about significant past events to the similar need for older adults with cognitive impairment to recall happy events long ago. Students are encouraged to think about the needs of the institutionalized older adult to live in an environment that is familiar and predictable, just as the well older adult they saw at home may have shown or expressed the importance of familiar and stable surroundings. Faculty cannot infer that positive attitudes toward the older functional adult living at home will automatically transfer to frail older adults with physical and behavioral impairments.

As students begin to make these transitions, their thoughts are exciting and profound.

I met a man who is so, who is learning to overcome the trauma of widowhood, who accepts the limitations of aging gracefully. He has helped me not dread aging so much. Knowing him has made me conscious of the tendency to stereotype elderly in the hospital as frail and feeble and unable to do much for themselves. Now, in the hospital, I try to see each patient individually.

A. W., CCP student

Students reminisce with the older adult; they develop a sense of history and recognize that each older adult has a meaningful life story to tell.

> *Mrs. P. is a survivor. Throughout her life, she has fought to maintain a sense of identity and autonomy . . . . Knowing Mrs. P. makes me realize that you can't just write off a very ill and unresponsive client. Every older person has a history filled with good and bad times. They may not be able to tell you, but they should be treated with respect and dignity.*
> Y. D. S., CCP student

Students begin to recognize the strength and wisdom of the older adult:

> *I met Mr. T. in his daughter's home. He is 70. He came to the U.S. three years ago, leaving behind his friends and his other family. He has learned to survive in an environment where he cannot even speak the language: like me, he is from Ethiopia. I learned to listen to him and really give attention to what he had to say . . . . After knowing him, my attitude toward older adults is changed. Knowing Mr. T. helped me realize that a sick older man I see in the hospital today was a healthy individual yesterday.*
> A. K., CCP student

> *Sometimes Muriel, who is 87, makes me feel ashamed; last year it seemed like too much for me to put up a little Christmas tree yet Muriel put up a real seven-foot tree that couldn't hold another ornament . . . . Muriel often refers to "older" people, people who are sicker than Muriel, or less mobile or less alert, but are Muriel's junior by as much as 20 years. People who seem "old" to me might not seem old to themselves. Age is truly just a number. We cannot judge people's capabilities by their age.*
> S. C., CCP student

ADDING A SECOND LEVEL NURSING HOME CLINICAL

When project faculty first envisioned a second level nursing home experience, they assumed that they would manage the four-to-five week nursing home clinical much as they did hospital rotations, except that in the nursing home, students would work exclusively with frail older adults.

But project faculty quickly began to realize that the non-acute care setting necessitated development of new practice patterns and new teaching methodologies. At first, the changes produced anxiety, frustration, and anger. The old rules for clinical education just didn't work. Resolution and transition of faculty to a new definition of the teaching role occurred as the differences between the two settings became clearer.

Dissatisfaction with the written care plan surfaced during the nursing home experiences. Instructors were troubled by students who wrote detailed care plans without addressing factors most relevant to the individual resident. One day a project faculty member, correcting care plans for fourth-semester students during the nursing home experience, wrote in bold letters across the top of a voluminous care plan, "Where is the person?" The limitations of the linear nursing process for addressing individual needs within the holistic perspective needed in the nursing home setting became apparent. Understanding the *lived* experiences of illness and frailty escapes the formalizations of the traditional nursing care plan approach (Tanner, 1988). Faculty began to search for ways to meet the need for individualization of care plans in the nursing home. As a result, in the nursing home, groups of student write care plans together for a large group of residents, and critique these care plans in post-conference. They ask each other, could I provide individualized care for this resident after reading this care plan? How can phrases like "be consistent" or "establish trust" be made more meaningful and specific for each resident? With this exercise and with continual encouragement from faculty and staff to generate unique interventions not described in a textbook, students begin to recognize the specific knowledge embedded in each clinical encounter. They realize that one cannot simply transfer broad interventions intact from one situation to another. If students are to incorporate a holistic, caring approach amidst the complexity and rapid changes within today's health care system, this understanding is essential.

Also, faculty began to realign power relationships between students and teacher. A series of questions emerged in our thinking: Is it not time for us to begin the practice of collegiality with students? To share care planning, for example, rather than asking second level students to prove to me each week that they are capable of rediscovering a plan of care? Why do students need to go in cold each week to assess clients, determine behavioral outcomes, and generate nursing interventions? Is it any wonder that they run out of time to individualize, to find the person? We concluded that in the nursing home setting students would be assigned the same group of residents for the entire experience. Each student shares at least one client with the instructor; together they conduct assessments, co-lead reminiscing activity groups, and brainstorm about creative approaches to care. For faculty, the nursing home experience has provided a paradigm to generate active, collaborative teaching approaches that are applicable in a variety of settings. Faculty have become colleagues and mentors. Students are given a better chance to be successful and to make a difference in the quality of another individual's life. This is the beginning of empowerment.

Goals of the Nursing Home Experience

Initially, faculty for the nursing home clinical thought in terms of diabetes, arthritis, dementia—med-surg nursing for older, frail individuals. But the nursing home was different, and those labels did not define the resident. We realized that the essential learning activity in a nursing home clinical rotation, coming at the end of the student's program of study, must include experiences that focus on nursing decisions within a care-oriented setting. The limitations of the acute hospital as a learning environment became clearer. Because the hospital is based on the medical model with its focus on cure, because technology is the primary form of intervention, and because the emphasis is on the physician as the key decision maker, it may not be the best place to learn care-oriented nursing. In time we made a startling discovery: We are in the nursing home precisely because it is not the hospital. The nursing home may very well be the best place to teach selected nursing concepts that are an essential component of nursing practice in all settings. Because the acute hospital has become such a fast-paced, hi-tech, short-stay, high stimulus environment, it has become a less effective teaching learning environment for some aspects of nursing. The nursing home, on the other hand, where nursing care is the critical variable in patient well being, provides the opportunity to learn functional and cognitive as well as physical assessment, make nursing decisions over time and evaluate their effectiveness, manage the impact of the environment on the resident's condition, work closely with nursing assistants, and set goals and carry out nursing interventions that maintain, or at best, rehabilitate, but do not necessarily cure.

Understanding how we arrived at this particular set of learning activities necessitates a discussion of the DACUM process. DACUM, an acronym for "Developing a Curriculum," is a process designed to assist expert practitioners in a designated field to identify essential competencies for safe and effective practice in that field. Sponsored by the W. K. Kellogg Foundation, 12 directors of nursing from national project nursing homes participated in a DACUM process for gerontological nursing. They generated a list which includes over 300 competencies within the 18 categories of essential clinical skills listed in Figure 6-1. In order to define essential curriculum content, faculty in project schools surveyed themselves to identify the appropriateness of each of the 300 competencies for the associate degree program. Each of the 300 competency statements were rated according to these questions: (1) What competencies are currently taught in your program? (2) What competencies need an increase or different emphasis in your program? (3) What competencies cannot adequately be taught in the ADN program?

Faculty showed agreement on competencies that cannot be taught within the four semesters of the AD curriculum, including staff-supervision, maintenance of equipment, and long-term planning for inservice offerings. Project faculty agreed that a large number of original DACUM competencies dealt with general nursing knowledge while a small percentage of the original DACUM competencies related specifically to the care of the frail older adult in the nursing home. Interestingly, the majority of DACUM competencies which were described by project faculty as "currently taught" in project schools nursing curricula relate to areas

Figure 6-1
Community College-Nursing Home Partnership

Initial DACUM Categories

Communicate effectively
Continue professional and personal growth
Exhibit management skills
Perform assessment of resident
Develop plan of care
Implement plan of care
Administer medication to a large group of residents within a limited time
Perform technical skills
Practice rehabilitation nursing skills
Document resident care data
Practice risk management
Practice infection control
Manage the living environment
Practice within legal parameters
Practice code of ethics
Respond to emergency situations
Educate others
Manage resident and family stress

of general nursing knowledge, for example, assessment, planning and evaluation, communication, and ethical/legal issues.

Further refinement of the DACUM list was still needed. While each of the originally identified DACUM competencies are seen as essential to provide nursing care to older adults, some competencies are specific to the nursing of frail older adults with multiple chronic health problems and potential or existing functional and cognitive impairments. These were named as specific competencies to be mastered by associate degree nursing students in order to be effective caregivers of frail elders in both the acute and long-term care setting. In addition, a new question was asked: Of these specific competencies, which ones are best taught in long-term care? There was agreement among the faculty members at the six project schools that the 22 competencies shown in Figure 6-2 are essential to care of the frail older adult and are best taught in the long-term care setting. Superficially, the 22 practice competencies appear common to all settings. On closer examination, however, it is clear that in the nursing home setting, where health promotion, rehabilitation and maintenance of quality of life for residents are primary considerations, there are special opportunities for mastery of these competencies. Faculty have incorporated these competencies into specific clinical objectives for students in the nursing home clinical.

Obviously, the identified competencies are not taught solely in long-term care; content on assessment, rehabilitation, and management are introduced prior to the second level nursing home clinical experience and are threaded throughout all nursing courses. But the nursing home setting, where nursing judgments about nursing care issues form the basis for practice and where students, staff, and faculty participate in a nursing model of care delivery, may very well be the best place to emphasize these basic nursing competencies. Yet for students to fully participate in making nursing judgments in a care-oriented environment, they require a certain level of maturity. The nursing home experience described here is designed to occur at an advanced level of student development because the ambiguity and complexity of providing health-promoting, holistic nursing care to frail older adults with multiple chronic disabilities necessitates a well-developed knowledge base in assessment, intervention, evaluation, management, and psychomotor skills.

Furthermore, the long-term care setting, with its emphasis on health promotion, maintenance, and rehabilitation demands that faculty teach the essential competencies from the perspective of a care-oriented setting. In this way, the nursing home clinical is not just another medical-surgical rotation but rather an essential learning experience for all students to

Figure 6-2
Community College-Nursing Home Partnership

Competencies Best Taught in the Nursing Home

Perform Assessment of Resident
Assesses current mental status
Assesses functional abilities (ADL and instrumental)
Differentiates normal aging process from disease process
Recognizes age-related differences in disease processes
Values goals that maintain optimal functional ability

Practice Rehabilitation Nursing Skills
Defines restorative goals
Elicits active participation of resident in restorative program
Facilitates choices to decrease learned helplessness
Promotes independence of ADLs
Initiates bowel and bladder training
Implements contracture prevention methods
Evaluates effectiveness of restorative programs
Implements group therapies (e.g., reality orientation, memory enhancement,
   reminiscing)

Manage the Living Environment
Allows resident to continue previous lifestyle to degree possible
Provides comfortable homelike environment for socialization
Plans room arrangement to facilitate resident needs
Reduces environmental stress (e.g., noises, isolation, lighting, roommate)
Provides opportunities for expression of ethnic and cultural practices for residents
Provides for sexual expression of residents
Initiates interventions to deal with combative residents
Assists families to cope with unrealistic expectations, guilt, and anger

Exhibit Management Skills
Adopts leadership style appropriate to situation
Delegates appropriately
Resolves problems utilizing problem-solving skills over an extended period of time
Updates plan of care

Editor's Note: The competencies are presented here as they were first developed; they
are in the language of nurses who work in nursing homes, and have not had the
polish that an educator's hand might place on them. In the experience of project
faculty, the pragmatic and straightforward expression carries force and usefulness. One
additional area of competency has emerged as being important to add: In the years
since the "best taught" competency list evolved, the ethical concerns and subsequent
legal issues which arise in care of older patients heighten the importance in nursing of
responding to the values and beliefs of each individual. Providing for informed
consent and self-determination when caring for the older person is seen as essential.

learn about the care of the frail older adult, to practice nursing in a care-focused environment, and to be empowered to provide new ways of caring.

THE COMPETENCIES "BEST TAUGHT" IN THE NURSING HOME

Exhibit Management Skills

The nursing home offers a variety of learning experiences to nursing students to prepare them for the manager of care role of the associate degree graduate. (Manager of care is one of three practice roles described for the ADN graduate in the 1990 NLN publication, *Educational Outcomes of Associate Degree Nursing Programs.*) In the nursing home, students collaborate with peers and nursing staff to effect mutually developed resident goals. Furthermore, students have the opportunity to care for residents over time and to evaluate progress; the focus is on interdisciplinary coordination of care for individuals with long-term, chronic care needs.

Throughout the project schools, the format of the nursing home management experience differs (see Chapter 4 for descriptions.) Examples of learning activities to meet management objectives are found in Appendix G. Collaboration with peers and nursing staff is an important component of the management role. The slower pace of the nursing home environment lends itself to this collaborative activity, and students learn a great deal about working together. Very often this is the students' first real collaborative experience with peers, or with assistive personnel.

Students also learn skills noted in the DACUM list, situational leadership skills, and delegation of selective nursing activities to other nursing personnel, particularly nursing assistants. Collaboration with LPNs in developing care plans and with nursing assistants in organizing basic care delivery is a key learning activity. Students find that delegating tasks and then being accountable for the safe performance of those tasks is new and not easy. They need continual faculty support and encouragement from staff to carry out delegation activities. The learning embedded in these encounters extends far beyond the specific nursing home experience; students begin to understand that the nursing assistant may not have the same knowledge base as the student, but that the student and the nursing assistant share the same values about caring and competence. One second level student relates:

> *I saw the nursing assistant take Mrs. P. into the bathroom for AM care in her wheelchair. But the wheelchair was too low for Mrs. P. to reach the sink and Mrs. P. just dripped water over herself as she tried to bathe. I thought, "How cruel; why would she set Mrs. P. up in this way? Mrs. P. can barely reach the sink." So I talked to the nursing assistant. She told me that she used the wheelchair because it was the only chair in the room that fit through the bathroom door. Actually, the nursing assistant was quite proud of herself for promoting Mrs. P.'s self-care which was the goal we had set for her. I realized that the nursing assistant didn't even notice that the wheelchair was too low. Together, the nursing assistant and I found a chair that was stable, and cushioned and high enough so that Mrs. P. could reach the sink. That morning, after Mrs. P. was bathed, I bought a donut for the nursing assistant and we had coffee together. She really tries very hard to do a good job with residents.*
>
> CCP student

Students collaborate with members of the interdisciplinary team to advocate for residents.

> *I cared for a resident with amytrophic lateral sclerosis. He developed difficulty swallowing. His wife came in to visit every day. Neither the resident nor his wife wanted the feeding tube re-inserted. I talked with the social worker and together we arranged for Hospice care in the nursing home. The feeding tube was not inserted. I felt good about being able to help him carry out his wishes.*
>
> Valencia student

The planning of care was identified in the DACUM process as a component of management. Because students care for the same group of residents for an extended period of time, they are more willing to explore creative and novel interventions and, most importantly, to evaluate the effectiveness of their interventions over time. Early in the project, we began to realize that in our curriculums focused on acute care, we develop wonderful "assessors," but often fail to educate effective "evaluators." Each week in clinical in the acute care setting, students assess a new patient and develop nursing diagnoses and goals based on that assessment.

But they rarely see that patient two weeks or even two days in a row, and can seldom implement and evaluate care plans.

We have learned the importance, during the nursing home experience, of emphasizing for students the opportunity to develop on-going care plans for a group of residents and make modifications as needed. Students are actively encouraged to collaborate with peers, staff, and faculty in evaluation and revision of care plans. The empowerment that emerges from this experience is compelling (Burke et al., 1990, p. 65).

On my first day in the nursing home, I noticed that one resident, Mrs. P., wasn't adjusting well. She was agitated, demanding, disoriented, and refused to eat. She laid in her bed and stared at the ceiling. She was being tube fed, had a Foley catheter, and soft wrist restraints. I introduced myself and she said, "What do you want with me? It doesn't matter, I have nobody. Just help me to die." I was totally overwhelmed and didn't know where to begin.

I went to her chart and saw that her medical diagnosis was listed as organic brain syndrome. She was a widow and a fairly new resident. She was receiving Haldol twice a day and Halcion at night. I went back to her room to assess her, but could find nothing physically abnormal.

As I bathed her, we talked. She told me about her parents death, the death of her husband, and the beautiful home that he had loved. She wasn't able to have children, and had no one left except a niece. The behavioral pattern that I was seeing pointed more and more toward depression rather than dementia. A nursing plan of care was formulated to increase her self-esteem by finding something to make her feel good about herself and to begin to accept her new home. She said she enjoyed cooking and crocheting in the past, so to start, I chose crocheting. Our student team brought in needles and wool and gave them to her. To everyone's surprise, she began crocheting. One morning, I came in to find that during the night Mrs. P. had pulled out her Foley catheter and fell trying to get out of bed. We talked about it and she said, "I'm not a baby; I can go to the bathroom on the bedpan."

Soon she began to eat breakfast in her bed and I brought her a newspaper each morning to read. One day she agreed to be taken to the day room by wheelchair. She was seated at a table with three other female residents who were eating their lunch. She looked up at me and said, "So, where's my lunch. I want what they have. Where's my beef?" Her sense of humor was an indication that her depression was lifting.

She began eating daily in the day room and socializing with her three new friends. The tube feedings were turned off. Our team worked together and helped these four women form a crocheting circle while talking and eating together. Mrs. P. began asking for the bedpan and the Foley catheter was not reinserted. After four weeks of being with Mrs. P., I began to feel that I was making a difference.

The last week of my clinical laboratory experience, I discussed with her the possibility of walking again. She was sitting in her wheelchair and looked up at me with surprise. She said, "Is that all you want? I can do that! Nobody ever asked me." With that, she got up and walked a short distance to another chair. I had tears in my eyes and that moment made me proud to be a nurse. Mrs. P. is walking again with the assistance of a physical therapist. She is gradually accepting her new home. And she is learning to balance independence with appropriate dependence while not becoming helpless. Her depression is lifting and the amount of Haldol she receives has been reduced. She is now more oriented throughout the day. I shall carry this experience with me throughout my nursing career.

CCP *student*

Another student talks about an empowering experience:

Every week, I noticed that Mrs. K. would fall asleep and slump in her chair from mid-morning to lunch time. Her weight had decreased over the past three months; I think it was because she never ate lunch and only picked at dinner. After a few weeks, I began to suspect that her daily insulin might be the cause. I talked with the staff and secured permission to obtain a blood sugar at 10 AM. It was 40. I called the doctor and talked to him about my assessment. He discontinued her insulin. The last week of the rotation, Mrs. K. joined our mid-morning group activity blowing bubbles and laughing with us. She has gained a pound. I really did make a difference in her life.

Perform Assessment of Resident

The significant learning opportunity in the nursing home regarding assessment skills lies in the opportunity for students to combine data from multiple sources in planning care. Students bring to the setting the ability to perform a complete physical assessment; in the nursing home they add the skills of cognitive and functional assessments and then relate all findings to normal aging processes and age-related differences in disease pictures.

We have found that it is important that students utilize standardized tools to assess cognitive and functional ability. This activity provides them with an opportunity to validate findings against standardized norms. It is difficult to recommend one test over another. Often, the tools were originally developed for different purposes, and fine distinctions exist among them. We recommend using standardized tools to assess functional ability, always encouraging the student to account for cultural and ethnic differences, fatigue, and environmental stimuli. Most project schools use the Folstein Mini-Mental State Examination (Folstein, Folstein, & McHugh, 1975; and see Appendix E) to assess cognitive ability and the facility's tool for determining functional level. For a full discussion of assessment tools and their use we recommend five sources; the first three are nursing texts, and the next two are medical texts which are helpful on this topic.

Chenitz, W. C., Stone, J., & Salisbury, S. (1990). *Clinical gerontological nursing.* Philadelphia: W.B. Saunders.

Eliopoulos, C. (1991). *Gerontological nursing.* Philadelphia: J.B. Lippincott.

Mateson, M. A., & McConnell, E. (1988). *Gerontological nursing.* Philadelphia: W.B. Saunders.

Busse, E., & Blazer, D. (Eds.) (1989). *Geriatric psychiatry.* Washington, DC: American Psychiatric Press.

Cassel, C., Rosenberg, D., Sorenson, L., & Walsh, J. (Eds.) (1990). *Geriatric medicine.* New York: Springer-Verlag.

Feil, N. (1989). *Validation: The Feil method.* Cleveland, OH: Edward Feil Productions.

Clinical objectives from CCP, found in Appendix I, illustrate use of findings from standardized assessment tools to help students plan care. Learning to assess cognitive and functional abilities requires time and continual guidance from faculty and staff. Based on their assessments, students are encouraged to develop resident goals to improve or maintain functional and cognitive ability in order to prevent secondary complications and delay further disability. Students also are supported in planning goals that assist individuals to decline or die with peace, comfort, and dignity. Typically, students focus on cure-oriented goals and interventions; in long-term care the internalization of chronic care goals can be difficult because it requires a different perspective on care norms and on the criteria for success. In long-term care, maintenance of functional ability, despite the presence of multiple chronic disabilities, can imply tremendous progress. It is important for students to gain this perspective, to advocate for maintenance of basic human needs, especially if they are to provide competent, health-promoting care to older adults in any setting. Two students who worked together as a team have written about a resident that became special to them:

> *We will never forget Martha, a resident who was always "on the go."*
> *She was never in her room. Martha tried to keep busy by helping other*
> *residents and reading but she felt she could do more; after all, she had*
> *worked for 40 years as a legal secretary and she was used to hard work.*
> *The more we knew Martha and after completing the functional and*
> *cognitive assessment tools, the more we knew that there must be something*
> *in the nursing home that she could do that would help her connect with*
> *her past and that would maintain her interest in being helpful. We discussed*
> *Martha with our instructor and we were able to set up an appointment*
> *with the nursing home administrator to discuss meaningful work for*
> *Martha. Martha is now dispensing mail to all the residents at the nursing*
> *home; she has become a vital member of the "nursing home team."*
> *Triton students (in Burke et al., 1990)*

Another student related how she refused to accept maintenance of functional ability at her present level for Mrs. B:

> *I saw that Mrs. B. did not interact with other residents. She ate in her*
> *room; she did not participate in activities. The staff told me "that's how*
> *Mrs. B. always is—she likes to be left alone." I did a complete assessment,*
> *including a mini-life history. Mrs. B. talked about her job as a second*
> *grade teacher and how she missed being with the children. I asked her to*
> *walk with me to the group room, to "just observe." Slowly, after a few*
> *weeks, she joined the group. The last week of clinical, she asked to eat in*
> *the dining room.*
> *Valencia student*

Practice Rehabilitation Skills

The nursing home provides an opportunity for students to plan care and embrace rehabilitation potential for residents despite the presence of functional and cognitive impairment and chronic illness. Specific learning activities in this area focus on skin care, contracture prevention regimes as well as active mobility programs, bowel and bladder training, and restorative eating programs. Goals are directed toward improvement of function. Students work together to plan creative, individualized care plans for residents who are appropriate candidates for rehabilitation. Faculty and staff assist students to define restorative goals that are realistic and developmentally appropriate. Students are encouraged to actively seek out rehabilitation potentials for each resident and combine these goals with strategies for maintenance of functional and cognitive ability and illness prevention to develop a comprehensive care plan. The fact that students conduct this complex activity over time and evaluate weekly outcomes contributes to their success in meeting resident goals.

A student speaks to her "success" in assisting a resident with restoration of continence:

Every morning, I would find Mrs. W. wet. She would holler and scream and refuse to eat breakfast. This was very discouraging to me. I began to wonder if being wet made her act this way. So I started going to her room, first thing in the morning, even before report and I would take her to the bathroom. She stopped hollering. She started eating her breakfast and gained a pound by the time I left. I always thought I'd want to work in the recovery room or ER—exciting, you know—but here you can really make a difference in people's lives.
CCP student

Another significant learning activity for students in the nursing home, is participation in a therapeutic group activity with residents. Students have the opportunity to develop a small group, choose the residents and the type of group activity (music, exercise, reminiscing, games, remotivation), and participate in the group over a two to three week period. (Burnside, 1986, is a valuable resource for faculty and students regarding group process with the elderly.) Frequently students are merely observers to group process. But in the nursing home, teams of students, sometimes with their instructor, actively lead a group and experience surprising outcomes. Students find rehabilitation potentials they never suspected: In our fourth semester, clinical groups are divided into teams of three to four students. Each team worked with the same group of residents to provide consistency in care.

After discussing the plans for our group activity with my team members, we decided to run a music therapy group.

When I think about the music group, two individuals come to mind. One was a 92-year-old woman, blind, hearing impaired, and severely contracted. Each week she would be brought to the group reclining in her geri-lounger, appearing oblivious to her surroundings. But one day, during music group, we noticed that she was responding to the music by independently moving the only part of her body she was able to—tap her foot! She was tapping it to the music.

The second resident I recall was an elderly gentleman who was a bilateral amputee with hands that were severely contracted due to a previous C.V.A. and arthritis. During our last music group, he rolled over to the piano and endeavored to play his favorite songs. He had worked as a piano player for 35 years, yet no one previously had been aware of his skills.

Somewhere during the music group our perceptions of the elderly and the issues we previously viewed as important changed; we no longer concentrated on the deficits experienced by the residents but on the individuals themselves, individuals with very unique personalities, all having lived full lives with many stories to share.

Obviously, students need tremendous encouragement from faculty and staff to persist in directing residents toward rehabilitation. Movement often is slow with incremental resident progress. Students and faculty are easily discourged. But we have learned something very important throughout the years of project activities in the nursing home. Students do not need many successes in finding rehabilitation potential and promoting optimal functional ability—only one. When they are given an opportunity to tell their story and recount their success, students will speak to their empowerment. They must have the chance to be healers despite tremendous odds, to experience that stunning human victory that is so integral to the caring mission of nursing. This crucial understanding may be "best taught" in the nursing home environment, where the focus is on care, maintenance, rehabilitation, and sometimes cure.

I will always remember Mrs. H. She had a massive stroke and, despite an extensive rehabilitation program, she had minimal mobility and her aphasia was really bad. I thought, "what kind of a rehabilitation goal can I write for Mrs. H.? She is so sad, and alone and there has been no progress." I did all the assessments we do in long-term care and I was still confused. My instructor encouraged me to find out what was most important to Mrs. H., right now. Reluctantly, I began to talk with her once again. When I asked the questions, she made a motion to wheel her down the hall to the staff refrigerator. When I opened the door, she frantically pointed to a Pepsi can. So I spent that day with the rehab therapist teaching her to say "Pepsi." And I wrote my goal, "resident will ask staff for a Pepsi each AM." Who would have thought that I would go through all this school and read all these books, and write all those care plans to write a goal about a Pepsi can. I learned so much from Mrs. H. Sometimes making a difference in a person's life takes patience and you may be uncertain about how to do it. But when you succeed, you feel really good.

Manage the Living Environment

The nursing home provides unusual opportunities for students to analyze environmental conditions and make changes that will enhance the quality of a resident's life. In the acute setting, the student has few opportunities to manipulate patient-environmental relationships and see the consequences of that action. But in the nursing home, students can identify coping styles that characterize successful adaptation to life in long-term care, assess the impact of variables such as noise and room arrangement, and observe the influence of ethnic, religious, cultural, and other group activities on the well being of residents. Because they are in the nursing home for several weeks, students can initiate interventions to foster a homelike environment and create a milieu that is therapeutic and builds self-esteem. In short, students have the opportunity to take control of the environment as a nurse.

Mrs. O. was very depressed when she returned from the hospital after a recent amputation. On her return she was placed on a skilled unit. Her roommate for three years had not seen her since her return. I arranged for a visit each day and incorporated the visit into both residents' plan of care. A very important and close relationship between Mrs. O. and her friend was maintained.
Valencia student

This student focuses on the need to reduce resident isolation. Sometimes, interventions are directed toward activities that influence the entire nursing home community.

I saw that new residents tended to stay in their rooms. So we designed a "buddy system" where experienced, ambulatory residents took a new resident under their wing and brought them to the dining room and to the group.

Both residents felt better. It amazed me that a simple idea like the buddy system would make such a difference; we reduced social isolation and we improved both residents' self-concept.

Although students are encouraged to work with nursing staff and other disciplines in assessing environmental variables and to make suggestions for change, this can be a difficult or frustrating assignment. Because resources are limited in the nursing home, they are primarily directed toward meeting basic resident needs, and environmental factors often are overlooked or ignored. Students are encouraged by faculty to focus on one individual, to solve one environmental problem at a time. Students need to experience success in environmental management at least once. Sometimes, the instructor will need to let the students brainstorm at post-conference and create the "perfect" nursing home where the physical, psychological, and social needs of the residents direct the physical layout of the home and influence the delivery of services. The essential key to learning is for students to understand that environmental factors clearly impact on resident well being and that the empowered nurse manages the environment to meet individual resident needs.

THE ISSUE OF ATTITUDES AND THE NURSING HOME CLINICAL

Fostering positive attitudes toward older adults has been a focus of nursing research (Tagliareni & Boring, 1988). There are a generous number of studies investigating experiences with the well-elderly as a catalyst for positive attitude development, and substantially fewer about attitudes toward frail older adults, specifically, older adults in the nursing home setting. At the start of the community college-nursing home partnership activities, many questions arose about what student attitudes would be toward a second-level clinical in the nursing home. Would their learning be diluted? Would experiences in critical care be more beneficial?

The answers are directly related to the program of learning. If the primary focus of the curriculum is acute care, and learning activities are solely in the hospital, then students and faculty will view a long-term care experience as "out of sync" and unnecessary. The question of the long-term care clinical becomes less of an issue when the curriculum provides the student with a sound knowledge base to care for the frail older adult and understand the paradoxes of health care for older adults in our technological, cure-oriented health care system. When early learning experiences set the stage for the nursing home clinical, and students are encouraged to broaden their concept of nursing, they view the experience as an enhancement of nursing knowledge and nursing expertise. As students practice in the nursing home and develop the knowledge and skills to be effective in that setting, they are gaining knowledge and skill that will make them effective caregivers for older adults in any setting.

The question of influencing attitudes comes up in discussing the use of the nursing home for clinical placement during the first nursing course. Traditionally some faculty have been concerned that exposing beginning students to frail older adults in institutional long-term care before they have any gerontological nursing background will foster negative attitudes and reinforce or induce stereotypical responses to old, ill adults.

A number of schools throughout the country, including two of the project schools, place students in nursing homes for a first semester clinical experience, as well as the second level experience . The focus of the first semester placement is on resident self-care abilities and needs, with the second year experience broadened to include planning and managing care for groups of residents and creating a therapeutic environment.

Still, even with the best designed curriculum and the most inspiring instruction, students often enter the nursing home and feel discouraged. They see insufficient staff, meager supplies, and antiquated technology. It is visibly different from the acute care hospital, and that difference is seen as negative. The deprecatory stereotypes about the nursing home and the nurses who work there are widespread, and students carry many of them. During the first week of the clinical rotation, many students have difficulty adjusting to the new setting. For the instructor, a primary objective in the first week is to facilitate open discussion about nursing practice in long-term care, encouraging students to verbalize their feelings, both negative and positive. Post-conference can be a difficult and lonely time for the clinical instructor, listening to students complain about deficiencies in the nursing home, hearing them yearn for the more exciting and, at that point in their thinking, challenging world of acute care. We have learned as teachers to be patient during this trying and unsettling opening week. With faculty support and guidance, as the days go along, the students change in what they see.

The nursing home is not a perfect setting. Students do not have to like it, and not all will. But they must, and can, understand the nursing home, and experience its mission to provide a caring environment where rehabilitation, maintenance of functional ability, and promotion of self-care or assistance with decline are nursing's privilege and responsibility.

CARRY-OVER TO ACUTE CARE

In the second-level nursing home experience, students have the opportunity to be healers, and to create a therapeutic environment in a non-acute, non-technologically oriented setting. They learn to promote rehabilitation potential, orient their thinking and care planning toward health maintenance, and to serve as advocates for frail older adults. These nursing actions, which we believe are best taught in the nursing home, transfer to the care of patients, particularly older adults, in acute care. It has become clearer to project faculty that supporting students in generalizing from the nursing home to other patient care settings is an important instructional responsibility, and the "transfer" of concepts should not be assumed. A creative Ohlone faculty member uses the following scenario when students are in the second-level nursing home clinical:

You are on duty as the charge nurse of the medical/surgical unit of a 250-bed hospital in a medium-sized city. A skilled nursing facilty nearby has had a gas leak and has been ordered to be evacuated immediately because of possible explosion or fire hazard. There are 58 residents of the nursing home, most of whom are being transported by private car by either family or nursing home employees. A few are being brought by ambulance. Twelve of the residents are going home with relatives; the rest are coming to your hospital. You have sufficient empty beds, but they are scattered all over the hospital (obstetrics, oncology, critical care, etc.). The nursing supervisor is swamped with administrative matters such as getting hospital privileges for the attending physicians, and she asks you to make plans for the reception of these patients. What are the important considerations? Incorporate what you have learned in the nursing home.

At some project schools, students return to the acute care setting for their final clinical rotation immediately after the nursing home experience. Emphasis is placed on discussing the impact of an acute exacerbation of a chronic health problem on functional and cognitive abilities. Specific objectives for the acute care clinical which follows the nursing home at one project school (CCP) are:

The student will:

1. Complete a total assessment (physical, functional, and cognitive) of an acutely ill hospitalized older adult with multiple chronic health problems.
2. Implement nursing care directed toward maintenance of optimal functional ability as well as intervening appropriately in the client's acute exacerbation.
3. Identify how the setting, ethical-legal issues, and the condition of the client influence nursing management.

Students are encouraged to consider issues of continuity of care when assessing functional and cognitive ability, and to foster maintenance of self-care despite changes in health status. One student's experience following her nursing home rotation speaks to this focus:

> When I arrived on the med-surg unit, I was told that my patient, Mr. R., would need to go to a nursing home because he was unable to learn how to empty his supra-pubic catheter. The nurse had tried to teach him proper drainage techniques, "but," she said, "he just became confused and tearful." Since I knew Mr. R. had lived alone in an apartment before hospitalization and planned to return there "to be with my friends," I decided to do a more thorough cognitive assessment. I met with him and we talked; I administered the Folstein slowly over the course of the evening and found he had excellent recall and was able to concentrate on an activity. He was fully oriented. During that evening and the next, Mr. R. and I practiced emptying the bag over and over again. I kept telling him how much confidence I had in him and how well he was doing. When I charted at the end of the night, I made sure to describe his progress.
>
> When I came back to clinical the next time, I learned he had been discharged to his home with referral to the community health nurse. I felt terrific. I look at older adults differently now. I don't accept statements about what they can't do. Being independent, living in an environment that is familiar and safe; well, that's so important.
>
> S. C., CCP student

Our understanding of the significance of helping students transfer learning from the nursing home to other more technologically sophisticated settings may be the most significant project outcome related to curriculum development. Project faculty now believe that students must be provided with the opportunity to make nursing judgments within a nursing setting and then utilize information and skills from the nursing home in other clinical situations, in other health-care arenas. Well-elder experiences and senior level nursing home rotations form the basis for truly knowing the older adult in a variety of settings and that movement into the long-term care settings, where the focus is on care, not cure, no matter how comfortable faculty are with the acute care focused curriculum, is essential to educate competent, empowered caregivers in today's technologically focused health care system.

REFERENCES

Bevis, E. O., & Watson, J. (1989). *Toward a caring curriculum: A new pedagogy for nursing.* New York: National League for Nursing.

Boyd, C. O. (1988). Phenomenology: A foundation for nursing curriculum. In *Curriculum revolution: Mandate for change.* New York: National League for Nursing, 65–87.

Burke, A., Shirley, E., Baker, C., Deno, L., & Tagliareni, E. (1990). Perceptions from the nursing home: How we can make a difference. *Imprint, 37,* 62–55.

Burnside, I. (1986). *Working with the elderly: Group processes and techniques.* Boston: Jones & Bartlett.

Folstein, M. F., Folstein, S., & McHugh, P. R., (1975). Mini-mental state: A practical method for grading the cognitive state of patients for the clinician. *Journal of Psychiatric Research, 12,* 189–198.

Kuhn, M., Long, C., & Quinn, L. (1991). *No stone unturned: The life and times of Maggie Kuhn.* New York: Ballantine Books.

Tagliareni, E., & Boring, G. (1988). Faculty, student, caregiver attitudes toward the aged. In *Associate degree nursing and the nursing home.* New York: National League for Nursing.

Tanner, C. (1988). Curriculum revolution: The practice mandate. In *Curriculum revolution: Mandate for change.* New York: National League for Nursing.

Appendixes

Appendix A
Examples of Student Learning Activities with Well Older Adults

A-1

STUDENT CLINICAL EXPERIENCE WITH A WELL ELDER

General Guidelines

1. Follow a relatively healthy individual who is 70 years of age or older.
2. Make six weekly visits lasting 60 minutes utilizing guidelines related to a specified area of focus.
3. Summarize each visit using the *"Summary of Visit with Elder"* form.
4. Contact faculty for problems that arise or whenever assistance is needed.

Week one

Topic: Communication

Objectives: Completing this clinical experience will enable the learner to:

1. Demonstrate therapeutic communication and interpersonal skills;
2. Recognize the value of attentive listening (since not all problems of the elderly can be alleviated);
3. Discuss special considerations for communicating with the elderly; and
4. Evaluate his/her own communication patterns.

Preparation Activities:

1. Attend Orientation and Instructions for clinical experiences.
2. View Life History Film—"Old Fashioned Woman" (49 minutes). Critique communication problems and effective efforts observed in the film. How could communication have been improved?
3. Review Practical Pointers to Enhance Communication with the Elderly.
4. Familiarize self with Life History Tool.
5. Review Interviewing Format.

Student Learning Experience:

1. Explain purpose, length, and duration of visits. Prepare for termination.

A-2

2. Ask but do not force individual to sign a student/client contract.
3. Practice therapeutic communication skills.
4. Begin life history interviews.

Handouts:

Practical Pointers
Interview Format
Caring Nursing Behaviors
Caring Communication
Life History Tool
"Summary of Visit with Elder" Form(s)

Discussion Guidelines for Use in Seminar Following First Interview:

1. Discuss impressions, general reactions, and feelings to your first visit.
2. Identify at least one communication barrier.
3. Identify at least one therapeutic communication skill utilized.
4. Describe your perspective of client's response to interveiw.
5. Identify the practical pointers you utilized when communicating with your client.

A-3

SUMMARY OF VISIT WITH ELDER

Due: _____

Your Name _____ No. of visit _____

Place of meeting: _____

Time: _____

Elder's age _____ sex _____

1. Description of the interview (include impressions, general reactions, and feelings about your first visit):

2. Identify one communication barrier:

3. Identify one therapeutic communication skill utilized:

4. Describe your perspective of the client's response to the interviews:

5. State any practical pointers you utilized when communicating with your client:

A-4

STUDENT CLINICAL EXPERIENCE WITH A WELL OLDER ADULT

General Guidelines: (For use with interviews with well-older adult on Weeks 5, 8, 9)

1. Choose an older adult who is 70 years of age or older who lives independently in the community. (The older person should not be a member of your immediate household but may be a family member).

2. Make 2 visits lasting 30–45 minutes. The 1st visit is scheduled for completion on Weeks 5, and the second visit is scheduled for completion on Weeks 8 and 9.

3. Utilize the Guide to Interviewing Format in packet prior to each interview.

4. Summarize each visit using The *"Summary of Visit with Older Adult"* form. Bring completed form to seminar each week. After visit #1, complete the summary form #1, after visit #2, complete the summary forms #2 and #3.

5. Contact a faculty member (N101) if problems arise as a result of the interview.

6. Ask the older adult to sign the contract (in the syllabus) for the two interviews. If they seem reluctant, explain that they have a right not to sign. If the person refuses, it will be necessary to find another older adult to interview. Make sure that you explain to the older adult that you are not capable of giving advice related to health issues at this time. Hand in the completed form to your seminar teacher on Week #5.

A-5
INTERVIEW PERMISSION FORM

Have this signed by your client and return it to your seminar instructor.

I, _____ , have on
this date, _____ ,
agreed to allow a Community College of Philadelphia nursing student,
_____ , to inter-
view me four times during the fall semester for the purpose of his/her
learning related to the development of more effective communication
skills and enhanced understanding of the developmental process of various
ages. The information obtained will be confidential and discussed only
with the instructor and small groups of peers engaged in similar interviews.

A-6

INTERVIEW

Seminar: **Interview with Well Older Adult #2**
Topic: **Adaptation to Healthy Aging: Defining Healthy Aging/Creating a Healthy Environment**

Week 8

Objectives: The student will:

1. practice beginning interviewing skills.
2. identify factors that influence the older individuals perception of health.
3. Describe characteristics of successful aging.
4. Identify environmental factors that enable the older adult to maintain independence at home in the community.

Preparation Activities:

1. Complete "Draw Yourself" Activity as a way to think about your own conceptualization of aging.
2. Ask yourself the following questions:
   (1) How do I define health?
   (2) What parts of me are healthy now?

Hand-outs:

Draw Yourself Activity

Discussion Guidelines for Seminar:

1. Describe the picture you drew of yourself as an older individual.
2. By what criteria will you judge your own "successful" aging?
3. Discuss the older individual's perception of health. What factors contribute to an adaptive, healthy life-style?
4. Identify factors that enable the older adult to maintain independence at home.

A-7

Guidelines for the Interview:

(Suggested questions to ask the older adult)

1. Describe a typical day.
2. How would you describe your health?
   What causes you to feel this way?
3. What factors in your life contribute to your health?
4. Tell me about your home and your neighborhood and what they mean to you.

   Summarize the living situation:

   —How long have you lived here?

   —If the older adult is in a new living situation ask the older adult what circumstances precipitated the change.

   —If the older adult has lived in the present environment for a long time, ask the older adult how he has managed to be so successful at home. What has helped the older adult to remain independent at home?

A-8

SUMMARY OF VISIT WITH OLDER ADULT
(to be completed for Seminar on Week 9)

Topic: Adaptation to Healthy Aging: Defining Healthy Aging/Creating a Healthy Environment

Week 8

Name _____ Visit No # _____

Place of Meeting _____ Sex _____

Age of Older Adult _____

1. How did the older adult describe "health" and "old age"?

2. What factors were described by the older adult as essential for a healthy adaptive life-style?

3. Discuss the older adult's home and neighborhood. What factors enable the older adult to maintain independence at home. Which ones are *most* important to the older adult?

A-9

DRAW YOUR AGED SELF

DRAW ENVIRONMENT YOU WISH TO HAVE

A-10

ASSIGNMENT

Your assignment is to conduct an in-depth interview with a well elder in order to learn more about the positive and negative aspects of aging and to use as a foundation for assessing sick elderly individuals.

1. Introduce yourself and the purpose of the interview. Obtain permission for the interview. Be aware of yourself and the interviewee for non-verbal clues about how you are both feeling. Be sensitive about tone, distance, posture and gestures. Try to use open ended questions because others may inhibit the flow of communication. Avoid judgemental responses; ask, instead, Was that o.k.? or, How did that make you feel? A few minutes before it is time to close the interview, allow the person to express any other thoughts, feelings or impressions. Thank the person for sharing time and experiences. Do not share addresses or phone numbers.

2. Summarize the interview below.

   Senior's age _____ Gender _____

   A. Describe the interview from your perspective: impressions, general reactions and feelings.

   B. Were there any communication barriers? What?

   C. Describe your perspective of the client's response to the interview.

   D. Did the beginning of the interview feel any different than the end? How?

Appendix B
Examples of Fact Sheets to Assist Students in Integrating Gerontological Nursing Concepts

B-1

FACT SHEET
URI's and UTI's

I *General Information*

A. The prevalence of UTI's and URI's in the aged is high. Broncho-pneumonia is one of the leading causes of death in this age group.

B. Risk Factors in the Elderly

With age there exists an increased vulnerability to infection. Four factors that influence the elderly's vulnerability to infection are:

(1) *Degenerative Changes*

a. UTI muscular strength of bladder decreases, leading to incomplete emptying of the bladder and increased amounts of residual urine, thus providing an environment for microorganisms to multiply.

UTI's in the elderly are often associated with benign prostatic hypertrophy, diverticula of the bladder, bladder stones, arteriosclerosis of the bladder and clinical instrumentation for diagnostic or therapeutic purposes.

b. URI—
Older adults are more susceptible to URI's as a result of a breakdown of anatomic defenses in the respiratory tract due to aging (i.e., increased rigidity of muscles and connective tissues, and rib cage; decreased vital capacity, decreased ciliary action, 30% decrease in respiratory fluids, and decreased effectiveness of cough mechanism) and disease states.

(2) *Age-associated Circulatory Changes*

Decreased arterial elasticity, increased peripheral resistance, and atherosclerosis result in a diminished blood flow and decreased availability of oxygen, nutrients, antibodies and immune cells.

(3) *Subclinical Malnutrition*

This is a significant problem in the aged population. Adequate nutrition is important in maintaining the integrity of the skin and mucous membrane and in the production of antibodies.

B-2

(4) *The Functional Capacity of the Immune System Deteriorates*

Specific changes include progressive degeneration of the Thymus (responsible for producing T-cells), decrease in natural antibodies, increase in autoantibodies, decreased response to antigens and reduced cellular and humoral immunocompetence.

C. Although most older persons are able to meet ordinary respiratory and renal function demands despite these changes, there is reduced efficiency in the following areas:

meeting demands under unusual stressful circumstances;
lower resistance to infections; and
greater difficulty managing an infection once one develops.

II. *Diagnosis*

A. The presenting symptoms may vary from the typical URI or UTI presentation.

(1) Pain such as the chest pain with pneumonia may be absent. When pain does occur it may be less severe and, in the confused client, easily forgotten.

(2) Confusion, restlessness, and behavior changes may occur as a result of cerebral hypoxia. Blood flow to the brain is decreased when blood is diverted to the infection site.

(3) An elevated temperature as well as other signs and symptoms of infection may be absent or late in appearing. By the time symptoms become obvious the infection can be in an advanced stage.

III. *Management Considerations*

A. Bacteriuria is common in the elderly, and there is some debate about whether to treat it if it is asymptomatic, which is often the case.

B. Nursing care for the geriatric client with URI and URI's is similar to that employed for the younger client. Close observation for subtle changes is especially important.

C. The aged should be cautioned against periods of inactivity and bedrest due to the high risk of URI's.

B-3

D. The Center for Disease Control recommends the administration of influenza vaccines annually and the pneumococcal vaccine once (this vaccine is thought to be effective for life) for persons over 65 years of age.

FACT SHEET
STRESS AND THE ELDERLY

I.   *Stress and Adaptation*

A. Changes in functional reserve

1. Normal aging changes result in a reduced functional reserve capacity of body systems in the elderly.

2. The reduction in reserve capacity limits the older adult's ability to adapt to stressors such as injury, illness or intense stress (physiological, social, or psychological).

3. Homeostasis is more difficult to restore and maintain in the elderly.

B. Reaction of the endocrine system during stress in the aged individual is affected by the following normal aging changes:

— Decreased ACTH secretion
— Secretory activity of the adrenal gland decreases, therefore less epinephrine and norepinephrine are produced during stress
— Less aldosterone is produced and excreted in the urine of older persons
— The secretion of glucocorticoids is reduced
— Gonadal secretion declines with age, including gradual decreases in testosterone, estrogen, and progesterones
— Ability of heart rate to increase with stress decreases

II. *Surgery*

A. Why do surgery on an 80 year old? The quality of life can be significantly improved in elderly adults who have survived this long. An individual who reaches the age of 80 can expect to live 8.1 additional years even though the average life expectancy is 74.8.

B-4

B. The elderly client is vulnerable to various surgical complications due to the reduced reserve capacity of major organ systems (cardiac, pulmonary, and renal). Additionally, many elders suffer from overt or subclinical malnutrition and are generally more susceptible to infection than younger adults. Surgical complications for which the elderly are at high risk include the following:

1. *Respiratory complications* include atelectasis and pneumonia, and may be related to reduced endurance/fatigue, debilitation from co-existing chronic illness, and/or underlying pulmonary disease.

2. *Cardiovascular complications* include CHF, dysrhythmias, orthostatic hypotension, thrombophlebitis, and embolism. The cardiac reserve capacity is already compromised in the older adult due to decreases in stroke volume, cardiac output, and coronary artery blood flow.

3. *Acute renal failure* is most often seen post-operatively in the elderly client with fluid/electrolyte depletion and/or pre-existing renal dysfunction. Other factors which may precipitate renal failure include extensive damage, DIC, and the administration of nephrotoxic drugs (i.e., aminoglycosides, polymyxin B, colistin, NSAIDs, chemotherapeutic agents, gold salts). Elderly clients are especially vulnerable to the aforementioned risk factors because of normal aging changes such as reduced renal blood flow and decreased glomerular filtration rates.

4. *Hypothermia* (temp. less than 96°F.) is a complication that the elderly are subject to. Decreased functioning of the thermoregulatory center (hypothalamus), decrease in subcutaneous fat, and circulatory changes (decreased cutaneous dilation) predispose elderly clients to post-operative hypothermia because of exposure to cold operating rooms, cold solutions (betadine), lack of covering, and use of vasoconstricting drugs (Dopamine, Levophed).

5. *Infection and sepsis* are potential post-operative complications in the elderly. The most common sites for post-op infection are the urinary tract, respiratory tract, and surgical wound. Four factors which influence the elderly's vulnerability to infection are:

B-5

a. *Normal Aging Changes*

Decreased urinary muscular strength of bladder and increased amounts of residual urine can lead to UTI's in the elderly. Additionally, UTI's in the elderly are often associated with benign prostatic hypertrophy, bladder stones/diverticula and clinical instrumentation for diagnostic or therapeutic purposes.

(1) *Respiratory*

Older adults are more susceptible to respiratory infections due to disease states and age-related changes in the respiratory tract (i.e., increased rigidity of muscles and connective tissues, and rib cage; decreased vital capacity, decreased ciliary action, decrease in respiratory fluids, and decreased effectiveness of cough).

(2) *Circulatory*

Aging changes such as decreased arterial elasticity, increased peripheral resistance, and atherosclerosis result in a diminished blood flow and decreased availability of oxygen, nutrients, antibodies, and immune cells to the surgical wound.

(3) *Immune system*

The functional capacity of the immune system deteriorates. Specific changes include progressive degeneration of the Thymus (responsible for producing T-cells), decrease in the natural antibodies, increase in autoantibodies, decreased response to antigens and reduced cellular and humoral immunocompetence.

b. *Malnutrition*

Overt and subclinical malnutrition are significant problems in the aged population. Adequate nutrition is important in maintaining the integrity of the skin and mucous membranes and in the production of antibodies.

B-6

6. *Postoperative delirium* is a relatively benign condition which is self-limiting. It often occurs in elderly clients—especially those in intensive care units, and is characterized by restlessness, irritability, and disorientation and may include psychotic behavior. Factors which predispose the elderly client to post-op delirium include pre-existing dementia, fluid/electrolyte imbalances, cerebral hypoxia, and drug interactions/adverse reactions. The ICU environment with lack of windows, frequent interruptions of sleep, and continual lighting (making it difficult to distinguish day from night) put clients at an especially high risk for developing this complication.

C. Management considerations
   1. *Pre-operatively*
      a. Elderly clients must be carefully evaluated prior to surgery to identify risk factors such as dysrhythmias, a recent MI, malnutrition, pulmonary insufficiency, and impaired liver or renal function.
      b. Pre-operative medication dosages should be reduced by one-third to one-half the amount that would be given to a younger person of the same size.
      c. Pre-operative nursing responsibilities related to the elderly client include assessing for loose teeth and padding bony prominences to protect from skin breakdown while lying on the OR table. The elderly are already at an increased risk for decraboti because of a decrease in subcutaneous fat and skin change (dryness, fragility).
   2. *Intra-operatively*
      a. Local anesthesia is preferred over general anesthesia in the older adult since general anesthesia depresses the already compromised cardiovascular and respiratory systems.
   3. *Post-operatively*
      a. Elderly clients generally require less pain medication postoperatively for comfort. Care must be taken to avoid overmedicating the elderly with narcotics because of respiratory depression and cough suppression which can lead to atelectasis and pneumonia. However, enough medication must be given so that incisional pain will not inhibit deep breathing and coughing.

B-7

    b. Care must be taken to avoid fluid overload when administering IV fluids to elderly clients because of their already reduced renal function and myocardial reserve capacity. However, the importance of hydration is not to be undermined. The nurse must keep in mind that the hypovolemia and hypotension in the elderly are poorly tolerated. Strict I & O is a must.

    c. Post-operative nursing care must be aimed at reducing the hazards of immobility. Early ambulation, meticulous respiratory care, optimal nutritional intake, and the prevention of decubitus ulcers are essential.

III. *Shock*

    A. Early signs and symptoms of shock in the elderly may be absent or late in appearing.

    B. Signs and symptoms of shock in the elderly may be atypical.

        1. Confusion, restlessness, and behavioral changes may occur due to cerebral hypoxia. Blood flow is diverted from the brain to other vital organs (heart, kidney).

        2. A "normal-range" B/P of 130/70 could be indicative of shock in an aged individual whose base line B/P is 200/100.

        3. Heart rate may be WNL—the ability of the heart rate to increase with stress decreases.

        4. Signs such as cold, clammy skin may be slow to appear because of functional changes in the endocrine systems (slower vasoconstriction in response to stress).

B-8

REFERENCES

Andresen, G. P. (1989). A fresh look at assessing the elderly. *RN, 52*(6), 28–40.

Burnside, I. M. (1988). *Nursing and the aged.* New York: McGraw-Hill.

Christ, M. A., & Hohlock, F. J. (1988). *Gerontologic nursing: A study and learning tool.* Springhouse, PA: Springhouse Publishing Co.

Eliopoulous, C. (1981). *Gerontological nursing.* New York: Harper & Row.

Mason, J. H., Gau, F. C., & Byrne, M. P. (1976). *Cowdrey's: Care of the geriatric patient.* St. Louis: C. V. Mosby.

Rousseau, P. (1987). Comprehensive evaluation of the geriatric patient. *Postgraduate Medicine, 81*(1), 239–249.

Steffl, B. M. (1984). *Handbook of gerontological nursing.* New York: Van Nostrand Reinhold.

U.S. Department of Commerce: Bureau of Census (1990). *American Statistical Abstract.*

Yurick et. al. (1984). *The aged person and the nursing process.* East Norwalk, CT: Appleton-Century-Crofts.

GERONTOLOGICAL FACT SHEETS

Objectives:

1. Identify age related changes commonly found in the older adult.

2. Describe the effects of age-related changes in the older adult.

3. Identify nursing implications as they relate to the care of the older adults.

4. List pharmacological and nutritional considerations when indicated or related to the older adult.

B-9

SLEEP PATTERNS IN OLDER ADULTS

Aged-Related Changes	Effect on Maintenance of Sleep Rest Patterns in Older Adults	Nursing Implications
• Increase in number of arousals after onset of sleep	• Sleep interrupted—person may demonstrate behaviors of restlessness, and irritability	Assess for insomnia which is a subjective feeling of poor sleep associated with daytime fatigue.
• Slight decrease in total sleep time	• Even though only slight decrease in total sleep time, elder's perception is that of "poor" sleep pattern	Assess behaviors of sleep deprivation: • increased irritability • decreased concentration ability • chronic tiredness.
• Decrease in Stage III and IV sleep which is the slow wave sleep/deep sleep	• Deprivation of phase of sleep which is thought to contribute to physical restoration	Assess effects of "sleep." Client may be physically and mentally tired even though total sleep time may be 8 hours.
• Decrease in rapid eye movement (REM) sleep in persons over age 85.	• Deprival of "dream phase" of sleep which is thought to contribute to mental restoration	Assess for changes in mental status, particularly orientation, memory (short-term and recall) level of consciousness, and irritability.

B-10

Sleep apnea occurs in ⅓ adults over age 65 • absent respirations for > 10 seconds • occurs greater than 30 times at time	Disturbs sleep, client presents with snoring, sleepy all the time, decreased attention span, decreased memory and increased irritability	Assess for behaviors of sleep apnea. Evaluate use of medication, e.g., administering hypnotics or other CNS depressants may be life threatening.
Nighttime disturbance related to visual and hearing deficits	Altered perception of night environment increases fearfulness, paranoia, insecurity, especially if new environment	Keep small light as a night light on. Use flashlight to shine on your face for hard of hearing, elders to lip read.

B-11

PHARMACOLOGICAL CONSIDERATIONS

I. *Sedative Hypnotics* (Benzodiazepines)
    Nursing Implications for Older Adults
    1. Observe for excessive sedation especially in elderly. May cause "sunrise syndrome" (increased confusion in the A.M. due to hangover effect). Lesser activity level during day, decreased functional abilities noted after taking Benzodiazepines.
    2. In elderly do not use for long term use. (> 30 days). If patient requests sleeping med, try plain Tylenol for its analgesic effects.
    3. Interacts with Cimetidine to increase sedative effects.
    4. Halcion is very short-acting and has less tendency to cause morning drowsiness. Only 4× recommended dose is enough for overdosage to occur. Rebound insomnia may occur for several nights after drug is discontinued.

II. *Sedative-Hypnotics* (Barbituates)
    Nursing Implications for Older Adults
    1. Reduce all doses in elderly. Benzodiazepines may be drug of choice for short periods of administration. Start with low dose and monitor for side effects.

III. *Anti-anxiety* (Benzodiazepines)
    Nursing Implications for Older Adults
    1. In elderly, there is decreased biotransformation in the liver which leads to higher blood levels of active drugs. Serax and Ativan are drugs of choice due to their decreased half-life and rapid excretion.
    2. In elderly, observe for excessive daytime sedation.
    3. In elderly, observe for a paradoxical reaction (i.e., agitation, restlessness).
    4. Monitor blood pressure due to potential orthostatic hypotension, at risk for falls.
    5. Because of long half-life and sedative-hypnotic effects, given small dose in AM & in PM, especially with elderly.

B-12

6. Excessive sedation in the elderly may cause increased risk of incontinence and problems of immobility, increased risk of falls.
7. Benzodiazepines tend to increase the effect of anti-hypertensives, anti-coagulants, and CNS depressant drugs.
8. In elderly, may cause symptoms of depression.

Nutritional Considerations

Food substance that contain trypophan (meat, milk, and lettuce) do induce sleep. Tea and coffee are stimulants; therefore their use should not be within 2–3 hours of bedtime. They also act as diuretics which may increase nighttime awakening due to nocturia.

To prevent going to bed hungry, a light snack is useful, but a heavy meal will most likely result in indigestion and increase sleep pattern disturbances.

REFERENCES

Ebersole, P. (1990). *Toward healthy aging: Human needs and nursing response.* St. Louis: C. V. Mosby.

Eliopoulos, C. (1987). *Gerontological nursing.* Philadelphia: J. B. Lippincott.

Hayter, J. (1985). Sleep apnea: Causes for concern. *Journal of Gerontological Nursing.* September 11(9), 26–29.

Kuhn, M. M. (1990). *Pharmacotherapeutics: A nursing process approach.* Philadelphia: F. A. Davis.

Muncy, J. H. (1986, August). Measures to rid sleeplessness: 10 points to enhance sleep. *Journal of Gerontological Nursing, 12*(8), 6–10.

Appendix C
Sensory Loss Simulation
Student Learning Activity

C-1

OLD AGE SIMULATION EXPERIENCE

Introduction:

This experiment in old age simulation is designed to acquaint students in gerontology with what some older people experience as a result of aging. Although there are differences and degrees of sensory losses and physical impairment from person to person, nevertheless, most older people are affected by the changes in the aging process.

The experience you are about to undertake is a traumatic one since you will be instantaneously transformed from a normal condition or with minimal impairment of sensory or physical losses to one of advanced stage. The decrements represent a person in the late 70's and older. The continuous simulation period of two hours of an aged condition should make a tremendous impact on your ability to empathize with older people.

I. *Objectives:*
    A. To focus on the problem of sensory and physical losses due to the aging process.
    B. To allow students an experimental simulation of sensory and physical losses in an actual situation.
    C. To describe and analyze the problems of sensory and physical losses endured during the period of simulation.
    D. To become empathetic and become more aware of older people's problems from this experiment.

II. *Problem Areas of Simulation Experience:*
    A. Limited vision.
    B. Impaired hearing.
    C. Touch sensitivity loss.
    D. Limited physical mobility.
    E. Impairment of hand usage.

III. *Materials Needed for Experiment:*
    A. Saran wrap or similar clear polyethylene material.
    B. Cotton balls or tissue paper such as Kleenex.
    C. Two Ace bandages (2½″ wide size) and old newspapers.
    D. Gloves (dishwashing or surgical).

C-2

IV. *Old Age Simulation Procedure:*

A. Wrap an Ace bandage around the right knee with a newspaper folded under to stiffen the joint (LIMITED PHYSICAL MOBILITY).

B. Wrap the left foot with an Ace bandage by placing a crumpled newspaper made into a ball under the foot (LIMITED PHYSICAL MOBILITY).

C. Fold a clear polyethylene material four times lengthwise and long enough to wrap around the eyes and head (LIMITED VISION).

D. Moisten cotton ball or tissue paper and insert into ears (IMPAIRED HEARING).

E. Wear gloves on both hands (TOUCH SENSITIVITY LOSS).

V. *Experimental Activities:*

Do the following activities after preparing yourself into old age simulated physical condition.

A. Walk about to experience the limited sensory and physical abilities.

B. Try to read a newspaper or other reading materials to sense the vision loss.

C. Look up a telephone number in the phone book.

D. Dial a telephone number.

E. Attempt to write a short note to someone and feel the effects of limited vision.

F. Attempt to cut a piece of fabric into a circle, thread a needle, and sew a button on it.

G. Simulate a decrease in tactile sensitivity by attempting to do the following:

—identify a coin without looking at it
—tie your shoes
—button a shirt
—buckle a belt
—grasp a small object (paper clip, button, coin)

H. Listen to tape for a simulation of hearing loss in the elderly.

Appendix D
Student Learning Activities for Examining Attitudes Toward Aging

D-1
ACTIVITY TWO

Case Presentation

At the beginning of this learning experience the learners are given sealed envelopes. A case presentation is used to introduce content on long term institutionalization of the elderly. A brief description of the individual is read to the learner.

Case presentation

The patient is a white female who appears her reported age. She neither speaks nor comprehends the spoken word. Sometimes she babbles incoherently for hours on end. She is disoriented about person, place, and time. She does, however, seem to recognize her own name. I have worked with her for the past six months, but she still does not recognize me.

She shows complete disregard for her physical appearance and makes no effort whatsoever to assist in her own care. She must be fed, bathed, and clothed by others. Because she is edentulous, her food must be pureed, and because she is incontinent of both urine and stool, she must be changed and bathed often. Her shirt is generally soiled from almost incessant drooling. She does not walk. Her sleep pattern is erratic. Often she awakens in the middle of the night, and her screaming awakens others.

Most of the time she is very friendly and happy. However, several times a day she gets quite agitated without apparent cause. Then she screams loudly until someone comes to comfort her.

Following the case presentation the learners are asked how they would feel about taking care of a person such as the one described.

After the discussion the learners are instructed to open the envelopes of the individual described. The picture is of a six month old baby!

The discussion continues on why it is so much more difficult to care for a 90-year-old person than a 6 month old with an identical description.

Ruskin, P. E. (1983, November 11). Aging and caring. *Journal of American Medical Association, 250,* (18), 2440. Copyright 1983, American Medical Association.

D-2

ACTIVITY THREE

A Parable on Life

The purpose of the following experience is to provide the learner with an avenue for exploring beliefs and feelings concerning the aged and the aging process. It is intended to provide a personal experience rather than be a purely cognitive approach. The primary focus is on consciousness–raising and positive attitudinal development.

Method:

1. Have participants sit in their chairs or on the floor in a circle; lower the lights.
2. Request that members spend two to three minutes concentrating on their breathing, freeing their mind of all other thoughts.
3. Very slowly, narrate the parable (see following sheet), telling participants to try to fantasize themselves as the flower, feeling each new movement of growth. Ask each person to be the flower.
4. After completing the reading, allow several minutes of silence, then reform the group.
5. The teacher/facilitator should then ask the participants if they would share their reactions and feelings.

   Discussion should be guided by the group.

   Questions that may be raised are:

   What did you feel when you were grown?

   Did you enjoy the comfort of being noticed by the bees?

   Were you able to feel your strength as you faced the sun?

   Did you find satisfaction in standing tall?

   Did you enjoy sharing your food and knowing others relied on you for support?

   What were your feelings when you knew you were changing—when your petals curled and fell?

   You could no longer stand tall. What were your thoughts?

   Did you notice the bees no longer visited? Did you consider why? What would you have wanted to say to them or ask them?

   Were you happy? What made you happy?

   Were you frightened? What frightened you?

   Did you react to the new buds? In what way?

   What would have felt comforting as you dropped toward the ground?

   If someone had come by you at this point, what would you have liked them to say?

D-3

A PARABLE ON LIFE

It is springtime. The ground is warm and moist. The earth is ready for new life. Deep down, roots are strengthening and growing.

The bud begins to ripen; it is deeply enclosed in its green protective covering—receiving all its food from the stem. It stays tightly closed.

Then the covering folds back and a tiny red bud protrudes. It is small and perfect—just starting to extend into the world . . . just beginning to smell the air . . . to reach out to the birds and other flowers close by.

Slowly the rose begins to emerge: The calyx bends back in support; the petals grow longer and begin to separate slightly from the body of the flower. There are bees to entice and a fence to surround.

Constantly, the bud blossoms. Petal by petal it begins to grow apart from the main body. Its lines of communication with the outside grow stronger; it needs less closeness. The petals are strong enough to stand apart and reveal a young flower. The stem is a strong support as the rose stands tall and notices the other flowers in the garden. Food from the main stem is shared.

Then comes the time when all the petals are free. They stand and face the sun—a sturdy rose, a rose making seed to begin the process of life again, a rose strong enough to bend with the wind and sway with the breezes, wise enough to take from the air and rain what is needed for life.

As life goes on, the rose changes. The leaves begin to lose their greenness; the petals turn back and curl; lines form and colors fade. The rose looks around at the others close by—petals are falling—buds are coming forth. The rose's own first petal drops off, the others grow weaker, the stem can no longer support the flower. The sun now feels heavy; the rose wilts and the bees no longer support the flower. The sun now feels heavy; the rose wilts and the bees no longer visit.

Petals shower down. The rain and wind become enemies; the petals now fall easily. The rose faces the earth now . . . the last petals drop to the ground, too weak to hold on any longer.

Down on the ground, they look up and see the birth of new buds, new flowers, new leaves—the beauty and hope of tomorrow's garden.

LaMonica, E. L. (1979, November–December) The nurse and the aging client: positive attitude formation. *Nurse Educator*, 23–25.

Appendix E
Student Learning Activities for Functional and Cognitive Assessment

E-1

CLINICAL DAY 4: FUNCTIONAL ASSESSMENT

Objectives: Completion of this experience will enable the student to:

1. Conduct a functional assessment on an institutionalized elderly client;
2. Identify the facilitating factors and barriers to independent activity in a nursing home;
3. Discuss the social, emotional, mental and physical impact of institutionalization on the client and his family;
4. Explain the purposes of various rehabilitation services (P.T., O.T., S.T., etc.).

Preparation Activities

1. Review concepts of health promotion, restoration and rehabilitation.
2. Familiarize self with functional assessment tool.

Student Learning Experiences

1. Perform functional assessment utilizing functional assessment tool.
2. Update Kardexes to reflect actual functional abilities (after consulting clinical instructor).
3. Observe at least one rehabilitative activity (O.T., P.T., S.T.) and/or care planning conference.
4. Be an observer during mealtimes and watch for:
    A. Conversation patterns;
    B. Assistance given to clients;
    C. Food sharing/avoidance;
    D. Staff-client interactions.
5. Complete at least one nursing diagnosis related to functional status.

E-2

FUNCTIONAL ASSESSMENT GUIDE

Handouts

Functional Assessment Tool

1. Bathing (sponge, shower, or tub):
   I: receives no assistance (gets in and out of tub if tub is the usual means of bathing)
   A: receives assistance in bathing only one part of the body (such as the back or a leg)
   D: receives assistance in bathing more than one part of the body

2. Oral care:
   I: brushes own teeth and/or cleans dentures
   A: receives assistance in putting toothpaste on brush or brushing teeth
   D: doesn't clean own teeth/dentures

3. Grooming:
   I: shaves, combs hair, applies make-up
   A: receives assistance in shaving, combing hair, and/or applying make-up
   D: doesn't shave, comb hair, or apply make-up

4. Dressing:
   I: gets clothes and gets completely dressed without assistance
   A: gets clothes and gets dressed without assistance except in tying shoes
   D: receives assistance in getting clothes or in getting dressed or stays partly or completely undressed

5. Continence:
   I: controls urination and bowel movement completely by self
   A: has occasional "accidents"
   D: supervision helps keep urine or bowel control; catheter is used, or is incontinent

E-3

FUNCTIONAL ASSESSMENT GUIDE

6. Toileting:
   I: goes to "toilet room," cleans self, and arranges clothes without assistance (may use object for support such as cane, walker, or wheelchair and may manage night bedpan or commode, emptying it in the morning)
   A: receives assistance in going to "toilet room" or in cleansing self or in arranging clothes after elimination or in use of night bedpan or commode
   D: doesn't go to room termed "toilet" for the elimination process

7. Feeding:
   I: feeds self without assistance
   A: feeds self except for getting assistance in cutting meat or buttering bread
   D: receives assistance in feeding or is fed partly or completely by using tubes or intravenous fluids

8. Mobility:
   I: ambulates or operates wheelchair without the assistance of another person
   A: receives hands-on assistance with ambulation or wheelchair mobility
   D: unable to walk 50 yards, use stairs, use wheelchair

9. Transfer:
   I: moves in and out of bed as well as in and out of chair without assistance (may be using object for support such as cane or walker)
   A: moves in and out of bed or chair with assistance
   D: doesn't get out of bed

Adapted from: Katz Index of Activities of Daily Living. (1988). *Handbook of geriatric assessment*, Aspen Publishers.

E-4

FUNCTIONAL ASSESSMENT

ADLS	I*	A*	D*	N/A*	Comments
Bathing: Tub					
Shower					
Sponge					
Oral Care					
Grooming					
Dressing					
Continence					
Toileting					
Feeding					
Mobility					
Walk on level surface 50 yards					
Stairs					
W/C mobility 50 yards					
Transfers					

* = Independent   A = Assistance   D = Dependent
N/A = Not Applicable

E-5

Activities

Spectator:

    Sports __   TV __   Reading __   Radio __
    Movies/Plays/Programs __

Participating:

    Cards __   Games __   Visit w/friends __
    Letter Writing __   Walking __

Hobbies/Creative Arts:

    Sew/Handwork __   Crafts __   Music __
    Dance __   Gardening __   Pets __

Other:

Are there any activities you no longer do which you might be interested in renewing?

E-6

POST CONFERENCE DISCUSSION GUIDELINES

1. Observe the environment of the nursing home.
   A. Name at least one facilitating factor of independent activity.

   B. Name at least one barrier to independent activity.

   C. Name two creative ways which could be used to promote independence in your client(s).

2. Name two activities your client(s) participate in on a daily basis.

3. How has institutionalization affected your client socially?

   Emotionally?

   Mentally?

   Physically?

4. State the purpose of the rehabilitative therapy you observed.

E-7
CLINICAL DAY 5: COGNITIVE ASSESSMENT

Objectives: Completion of this experience will enable the student to:

1. Conduct a cognitive assessment utilizing the Folstein Mini-Mental State Exam;
2. Utilize the nursing process to develop a plan of care to improve (if possible) and/or maintain cognitive ability in an older adult;
3. Identify factors affecting cognitive ability in the older adult.

Preparation Activities

1. Read article: "Alterations in Thought Process."
2. Familiarize self with the Folstein Mini-Mental State Exam.
3. Pre-conference: Role-play on administration of Mini-Mental State Exam.

Student Learning Experiences

1. Predict results of Mini-Mental State Exam (WNL vs dementia) prior to administration, and then compare to actual findings.
2. Perform cognitive assessment on assigned client(s) using the Folstein Mini-Mental State Exam. Don't forget to give "clues" to your client(s) in AM before beginning exam.
3. Complete at least one nursing diagnosis related to mental status.
4. Prepare client(s) for termination of the therapeutic relationship.
5. Observe hall-sitting:
   A. How long do the residents sit without shifting?
   B. How many are restrained? Why?
   C. How many times are they touched without a task being performed?
   D. How many actually get a chance for conversation beyond the, "Hi, how are you?"
6. Observe one social/recreational group activity.

Handouts

Journal Article: Hall, G. R. (1988). Alterations in thought process. *Journal of Gerontological Nursing, 14,* (3).

Folstein Mini-Mental State Exam

E-8

INSTRUCTIONS FOR ADMINISTRATION OF FOLSTEIN MINI-MENTAL STATE EXAMINATION

Orientation

1. Ask for the date. Then ask specifically for parts omitted, i.e., "Can you also tell me what season it is?" One point for each correct.
2. Ask in turn "Can you tell me the name of this hospital?" (town, country, etc.).

Registration

Ask the patient if you may test his memory. Then say the names of 3 unrelated objects, clearly and slowly, about one second for each. After you have said all three, ask him to repeat them. This first repetition determines his score (0.3) but keep saying them until he can repeat all 3, up to 6 trials. If he does not eventually learn all three, recall cannot be meaningfully tested.

Attention and Calculation

Ask the patient to begin with 100 and count backwards by 7. Stop after 5 subtractions (93, 86, 79, 72, 65). Score the total number of correct answers.

If the patient cannot or will not perform this task, ask him to spell the word "world" backwards. The score is the number of letters in correct order. For example, dlrow = 5, dlorw, = 2. If the patient will attempt even a single subtraction, score the serial sevens in preference to the spelling task.

Recall

Ask the patient if he can recall the 3 words you previously asked him to remember. Score 0–3.

Language

- Naming: Show the patient a wrist watch and ask him what it is. Repeat for pencil. Score 0–2.

E-9

- Repetition: Ask the patient to repeat "No if's, and's or but's" after you. Allow only one trial. Score 0 or 1.
- 3-Stage Command: Give the patient a piece of plain blank paper and repeat the command. Score 1 point for each part correctly executed.
- Reading: On a blank piece of paper print the sentence "Close your eyes" in letters large enough for the patient to see clearly. Ask him to read it and do what it says. Score 1 point only if he actually closes his eyes.
- Writing: Give the patient a blank piece of paper and ask him to write a short sentence for you. Do not dictate a sentence; it is to be written spontaneously. It must contain a subject and a verb and be sensible. Correct grammar and punctuation are not necessary.
- Copying: On a clean piece of paper, draw intersecting pentagons, each side about 2.5 cm, and ask him to copy it exactly as it is. All 10 angles must be present and 4 lines intersect, as in the example, to score 1 point. Tremor and rotation are ignored.

Estimate the patient's level of sensorium along a continuum, from alert on the left to coma on the right.

From: DePaulo, J. R., Folstein M., & Gordon B. (1980). Psychiatric screening on a neurological ward. *Psychological Medicine, 10,* 125–132.

E-10

ITEMS OF MINI-MENTAL STATE EXAMINATION

Maximum
Score

	Orientation
5	What is the (year) (season) (date) (day) (month)?
5	Where are we (state) (county) (hospital) (floor) (city)?
	Registration
3	Name three objects: One second to say each. Then ask the patient all three after you have said them. Give one point for each correct answer. Repeat them until he learns all three. Count trials and record number.
	Number of trials
	Attention and calculation
5	Begin with 100 and count backwards by 7 (stop after five answers). Alternatively, spell "world" backwards.
	Recall
3	Ask for the three objects repeated above. Give one point for each correct answer.
	Language
2	Show a pencil and a watch and ask subject to name them.
1	Repeat the following: "No 'if's,' 'and's,' or 'but's.' "
3	A three-stage command, "Take a paper in your right hand; fold it in half and put it on the floor."
1	Read and obey the following: (show subject the written item). CLOSE YOUR EYES
1	Write a sentence.
1	Copy a design (complex polygon as in Bender-Gestalt).
30	Total score possible

Adapted from: Folstein, M. F., Folstein, S., & McHugh, P. R. (1975). Mini-mental state: A practical method for grading the cognitive state of patients for the clinician. *Journal of Psychiatric Research, 12,* 189–198. With permission of Pergamon Press, Inc. Copyright © 1975.

SCORING: *Scores of 23 or less: a high likelihood of dementia.*
Scores of 25–30: normal aging or borderline dementia.

E-11
POST CONFERENCE DISCUSSION GUIDELINES

1. a. State results of Folstein Mini-Mental State Exam.

   b. How did results compare to your prediction?

2. Identify at least two factors (positive or negative) which affect your client's cognitive function.

3. What specific goals and interventions have you written for your client (related to cognitive function)?

4. a. Discuss general reactions, impressions, and feelings about the observation of hall sitting.

   b. What changes, if any, might be implemented?

5. a. Which group activity did you observe?

   b. What purpose did that particular activity serve?

Appendix F
Student and Faculty Discussion Guides:
Polypharmacy in the Elderly

F-1

SEMINAR: POLYPHARMACY: REST/EXERCISE/ELIMINATION

Objectives: At the end of the seminar the student will:

1. Identify the major classifications of drugs described in the case study.
2. Identify the therapeutic action of the drug classifications described in the case study.
3. List side–effects common to the drug classifications.
4. Identify potential interactions that may result from the combination of drug classifications.
5. Identify nursing implications related to the administration of medications from multiple drug classifications.

Case Study:

Ms. Geraldine French, a 83 year–old widow, who lives at home with her 78 year–old sister and a grand–niece, is admitted to the orthopedic unit for an internal fixation of a fractured left hip. On the 6th post–operative day, Laura Jones S.N.C.C.P. is assigned to Ms. French. The team leader reports that Ms. French started physical therapy 3 days ago and has already begun weight bearing on the affected leg. She has been on a regular diet for 4 days; IV's were discontinued and Ms. French's I & O from yesterday was 850 Intake–1,250 output. The team leader reports that Ms. French continues to complain of pain and was medicated yesterday at 12 noon, 8 PM and 2 AM this morning with Demerol. The team leader asks Laura to assess Ms. French's affect; she reports that Ms. French has become increasingly lethargic, sleeping at long intervals during the day. Over the past 2 days, Ms. French has become weepy and expressed concerns about "never being well again." The doctor was notified of this yesterday and last night wrote an order to begin Ascendin 50mg BID today. Ms. French has taken Xanax 1mg at HS for chronic anxiety since her husband's death 6 years ago.

When you enter Ms. French's room, you find Ms. French sitting up in bed crying. She asks "What time of the day is it, dear? I am so mixed up. When I am home with my sister and grand–niece I wake up early and start the day fine. But here I feel like I'm in a fog. Right now I feel dizzy. And the pain doesn't stop. I'm afraid I'll never go home again and be with my sister." Vital signs are: 98.6–82–20, BP 100/60. Lung sounds are clear in all lobes. Peripheral pulses palpable. Skin warm and intact.

F-2

Laura returns to the nurses station and reviews Ms. French's medical history and drug orders. Laura noted a history of diabetes maintained with an oral hypoglycemic agent and a 1800 calorie ADA diet. Otherwise, the history and physical reveals that Ms. French has been in relatively good health. She has a slight hearing loss (she wears a hearing aid in her left ear) and mild arthritis in her knees. Ms. French reported that she often has stiffness in her knees and shoulders and takes Butazolidin 2–3 times a day while at home. Admitting vital signs are 98.6–88–24, BP 130/80.

When reviewing Ms. French's drug orders since admission, Laura notes that Ms. French's narcotic has been decreased from Demerol 75mg q 3–4 hours prn to Demerol 25mg q 4–6 hours prn with a new order two days ago for Tylenol #3 q 4–6 hours prn for mild pain. (Ms. French has not yet received the Tylenol). Laura also noted that Ms. French had been treated with Ancef 500mg q 6° for 5 days post–op. She is now on Velosef 250mg PO q 6°. Laura observes that there are orders for Colace, 100mg at bedtime; Metamucil, 2 tsp BID prn, soapsuds enema prn and paragoric, 10ml q 3–4 hrs prn and each had been administered at least once in the previous 48 hours. Review of the nurses' notes revealed how Ms. French came to have this regimen. The physician routinely ordered Colace after this surgical procedure. On the second post–op day, Ms. French had begun to worry about constipation even though she had advanced only to a full liquid diet and the physician ordered Metamucil at the client's request, since she had used the drug routinely at home. On the 4th post–op day, Ms. French complained of diarrhea and the night nurse phoned the physician, received the paragoric order and withheld the Colace. Yesterday, Ms. French complained of being constipated and a "feeling of fullness" and requested an enema, as had been her habit at least once a week before hospitalization. The record showed that she had also received Metamucil yesterday.

When Laura talked with Ms. French about her elimination status, Ms. French revealed that she thought "normal" bowel habits were essential to health and that one well-formed stool daily was the only "normal" pattern. Any deviation was termed "constipation" and "diarrhea" and promptly treated by Ms. French.

Ms. French's current medication orders are as follows:

Tolbutamide (Orinase) 0.5mg QD (8 AM)
Velosef 250mg q 6° P.O. (12 AM–6 AM–12 PM–6 PM)
Xanax 0.5mg BID (8 AM–10 PM)

F-3

Ascendin 50mg BID P.O. (10 AM–6 PM)
Maalox 30cc pc. and H.S. (9 AM–1 PM–6 PM–10 PM)
Colace 100mg gHS (10 PM) (Hold)
Metamucil 2 tsp. BID PRN
Paragoric 10ml q 3–4 hours PRN
SSE PRN
Demerol 25mg IM or PO q 4–6 hours PRN
Tylenol #3 1 tab q 4–6 hours PRN for mild pain
Dalmane 30mg qHS PRN

SEMINAR ASSIGNMENT: DISCUSS THE CASE STUDY AND UTILIZE THE FOLLOWING QUESTIONS AS GUIDELINES

1. What major drug classifications are included in Ms. French's medication regimen?

2. What other medications are included in these classifications?

3. What therapeutic effect is expected from the medications that Ms. French is prescribed?

4. What side effects can you expect from the medications Ms. French is taking? Based on the information in the case study, does Ms. French demonstrate any of these side effects?

5. What potential drug interactions could result from Ms. French's medication regimen?

6. What nursing actions are indicated in regard to Ms. French's medications and current clinical situation?

F-4

FACULTY GUIDE: SEMINAR: POLYPHARMACY: REST/EXERCISE ELIMINATION
(See objectives and case study on the student handout)

Discussion Questions:

1. What major drug classifications are included in Ms. French's medication regimen?

2. What other medications are included in these classifications?

3. What therapeutic effect is expected from the medications that Ms. French is prescribed?

   Utilize faculty guide re: Mechanism of Action to facilitate discussion.

4. (a) What side–effects can you expect from the medications Ms. French is taking?

   Utilize the Drug Classification Guide for the following drug classifications to answer questions 1, 2, 4a:

   Tolbutamide—Oral Hypoglycemic Agent (side–effects will be covered under interactions).
   Velosef—#21 Antimicrobial
   Xanax—#3 Benzodiazepines
   Ascendin—#18 Antidepressants (Tricyclic)
   Maalox—#20 Antacids
   Colace
   Metamucil⎰ #22 Cathartics and laxatives
   Paragoric—#23 Antidiarrheal
   Demerol—#7 Analgesics (Narcotic)
   Tylenol—#8 Analgesics (Non–Narcotic)
   Dalmane—#1 Sedative–Hypnotic
   Butazolidin—#6 NSAID (by History)

4. (b) Based on the information in the case study, does Ms. French demonstrate any of these side effects?

F-5

A. Lethargy, sleeping at long intervals, and confusion in the AM may be related to excessive sedation from the Benzodiazepine (Xanax). Because the Benzodiazepines are highly protein bound and complete with other protein bound drugs (NSAID's) for sites, the serum ½ life may be prolonged leading to exaggerated side effects. Also, impaired liver function may decrease drug metabolism. Dalmane may also contribute to hangover and confusion.

B. Weepiness and statement "I'll never be well again" may be related to long–term use of Benzodiazepines which may cause symptoms of depression. Also, narcotics may cause symptoms of depression in the elderly. These changes in affect are also intensified by current stressors, i.e. loss of mobility, fear of loss of independence, pain and uncertainty about the future.

C. Hypotension (130/80→ 100/60) and dizziness may be related to excessive use of a CNS depressant (Narcotics). Also, Benzodiazepines tend to increase the effects of CNS depressant drugs.

D. Aminoglycosides may contribute to auditory nerve damage, especially when there is a pre–existing hearing impairment. Although Ms. French is on a cephalosporin (Velosef) which is not as ototoxic, changes in auditory status should be assessed.

E. Ms. French's "seesaw" pattern in bowel habits is caused by misuse of cathartics and anti–diarrheals in the hospital and chronic laxative abuse by history. This side effect of excessive use of cathartics needs to be corrected. Also, the narcotic analgesic (Demerol) may be contributing to decreased peristalsis.

5. What potential drug interactions could result from Ms. French's medication regimen?

A. When highly bound protein drugs are taken by one client, toxicity may result. For example, NSAID's may increase the effects of oral hypoglycemic agents. Benzodiazepines are also highly protein bound and may alter the effects of NSAID's and tricyclic antidepressants.

B. The tricyclic and antidepressants may increase the effects of sedatives, tranquilizers and other CNS depressants. Therefore, as Ms. French starts on Ascendin, she needs to be observed for sedation, hypotension and increased confusion.

F-6

C. Maalox use may decrease the absorption of drugs taken within 1–2 hours, i.e. Velosef and Xanax.

D. "Sunrise Syndrome" (increased confusion in the elerly in the AM) may result from the hangover effect of drugs (i.e. Dalmane, Xanax, CNS depressants) and from early morning hypoglycemia.

6. What nursing actions are indicated in regard to Ms. French's medications and current clinical status?

A. Assess Ms. French's pain status. Since she is experiencing hypotension and excessive sedation which places her at high risk for falls and increased confusion, the nurse could question use of the narcotic analgesic. Perhaps Tylenol gr X on a q 4 schedule, planned around P.T. and activity schedules could be investigated. Talk with physician about Butazolidin use at home. Should it be restarted now since its use was effective for Ms. French. Talk with Ms. French about her fears with mobility and use of the affected hip which may be increasing her anxiety and negating the effects of the analgesic.

B. Xanax is a long–acting Benzodiazepine. Serax and Ativan have a decreased half–life and more rapid excretion and may be a better choice of anti–anxiety agent for Ms. French. This may decrease the excessive sedation. Give the entire dose at H.S.

C. Assess Ms. French's affect. Is the Ascendin necessary since the drug may contribute to hypotension, lethargy and further confusion? If the physician decides to continue with the Ascendin, the nurse should observe for behaviors that would indicate improved self–esteem and decreased sadness. The therapeutic effect of most tricyclics is prolonged in the elderly; however ascendin may act more quickly (4–7 days). Assess for an idiosyncratic effect, i.e. hallucinations, agitation and insomnia.

D. Change the medication schedule to allow for 2 hours between Maalox and the administration of other PO meds.

   i.e. Velosef (4 AM–10 AM–4 PM–10 PM)
       Maalox (8 AM–12 PM–6 PM–12 AM if necessary)
       Xanax 1.0mg (8 PM)
       Ascendin (6 AM or 10 AM–10 PM)
       Tolbutamide (6 AM)

F-7

E. Discuss with the physician the need to discontinue all cathartics and anti–diarrheals. Teach Ms. French about the cause and danger of laxative abuse, the role of diet, exercise and fluids in control of elimination. Restart Colace and/or Metamucil if necessary. Discuss with the client that a bowel movement every two–three days may be adequate. Note: even though Ms. French's bowel habits can be changed within the hospital, Ms. French may return to her former bowel habits when she returns home.

Appendix G
Example of Objectives for Management Experience in the Nursing Home

G-1
MANAGEMENT PRACTICUM

Activities	*Objectives*		
1. Meds and treatments for group	1. Passes medications safely to a group of residents	____	____
	2. Safely carries out treatments as ordered for a group of residents	____	____
2. Admission assessment	3. When possible, assists with an admission assessment	____	
3. Care Conf.—care plan revision	4. Participates in a patient care conference	____	
	5. Revises the nursing care plan for at least one resident	____	
	6. Confers with physician regarding care needs of a specific resident	____	
4. Team management and supervision	7. Makes assignments for nursing assistants on at least two days	____	____
	8. Monitors progress of nursing assistants in providing care	____	____
	9. Evaluates care provided by nursing assistants	____	____
	10. Provides feedback to nursing assistants regarding care given	____	____
	11. Formulates and presents to supervisor report on unit residents	____	____
	12. Communicates unit problems or concerns to supervisor	____	____
5. Staff teaching	13. Carries out a teaching project for staff	____	____
6. Evaluation	14. Completes a self-assessment	____	____

G-2

FOCUS: NURSING MANAGEMENT

Teamwork/Shift Report
Priority-setting/Decision-making
Delegation
Staff Development

Required Preparation:

S & L: Chapter 4, Team Approach to Nursing Care

Tappen: Chapter 18, 368–376 (teamwork)
Chapter 23 (staff development)

Supplemental Preparation:

R & B: Section 4, Units 13–18, Leadership Skills for Managing a Resident Unit

Key Concepts:

motivation
responsibility
accountability
authority
priorities
delegation
assertiveness
time management

Student Objectives:

1. Identifies five basic needs as motivators of individual employees.
2. Describes the advantages and disadvantages of team approaches to work.
3. Makes appropriate and fair staffing assignments based on case example.
4. Identifies the characteristics of a climate of growth for employees and discusses ways that a professional nurse can foster staff development.
5. Lists strategies to assist in avoiding burn-out.

G-3

6. Describes and critically analyzes the roles of the director of nurses, staff developer, staff nurse and nurse practitioner in long-term care settings.
7. Defines delegation and describes the flow of responsibility, authority and accountability.
8. Discuss ways in which priorities are set. Set reasoned priorities for a case study example.

Thought Questions:
1. Can you motivate another individual? If so, how? If not, why?
2. If you were director of nursing (DON) in long-term care, how would you foster an atmosphere of teamwork in your facility?
3. If you were a staff developer in long-term care, how would you move beyond teaching the ten mandatories and the inservices needed for recertification of nursing assistants.
4. What is the responsibility of the RN supervisor or DON when a corporate owner of a long-term care facility sets the nursing budget too low for adequate staffing?
5. What would you look for in selecting an RN for a team-leader position in long–term care?

Appendix H
Sample Learning Activities:
Ethical and Legal Issues

H-1

FACULTY GUIDE INVOLVING RESIDENTS

Activity Five: Role Play, "The Right to Fall?" (35 to 45 minutes total)

Introduction (5 minutes to divide into groups and read instructions)

All of the students will do the role play in small groups. The role play can be done with either three or four roles.

Divide the students into groups of three by having them count off aloud. The first person is #1, the second is #2, the third is #3, the fourth is #1, and so on. If there are one or two "extras," have each one join a group as a #4.

Distribute the handout "Role Play: The Right to Fall?" from their packets. Then distribute copies of the instructions for each player to the appropriate players (Mrs. L. to the #1's, Mrs. M. to the #2's, Miss N. to the #3's, and Mrs. P. to the #4's).

Go over the instructions to be sure that everyone understands them. Then tell them that they will have 15 or 20 minutes for the role play action.

H1 to H7 From: *Enhancing resident autonomy in nursing homes: Resource materials for nurse education,* by Debra David, PhD, San Jose State University, Martha Pelaez, PhD, Florida International University, and Gail Cobe, MSN, Ohlone College. Mimeograph.

H-2

ROLE PLAY: THE RIGHT TO FALL?

The parts: 1. Mrs. L., the resident.
2. Mrs. M., the nurse.
3. Miss N., the social workers.

(If your group has four members):
4. Mrs. P., the physical therapist.

The situation:

Mrs. L. is very unsteady on her feet because of Parkinson's disease. Based on an evaluation, the physical therapist has recommended a walker. The therapist fitted her with a walker and taught her how to use it. However, she refuses to use it. She sometimes uses a cane and sometimes walks without it.

Mrs. L. has fallen three times in the past two weeks, twice when using the cane and once when walking without it. None of the falls has caused more than minor bruises. Staff and family members are concerned that she will injure herself more seriously and want her to use the walker.

Action:

You are meeting to discuss the situation and negotiate a solution that will be acceptable to everyone.

H-3

ROLE PLAY: INSTRUCTIONS TO PLAYERS

(Cut along lines. Give each player instructions for her/his role only.)

Mrs. L.— You do not want to use the walker. In your view, it means "giving up." It's important to you to be independent and mobile. The walker is very slow and awkward, especially in the crowded hallways. Although you know that you are likely to fall again, you'd rather take the risk of some bumps and bruises.

Mrs. M.— You feel strongly that Mrs. L. should use the walker because of the risk of major injury. You think that Mrs. L. does not realize how serious a hip fracture or other serious injury could be. Also, you are concerned that surveyors will cite your facility for poor care if Mrs. L. is injured after repeated falls.

Miss. N.—You have mixed feelings about this situation. On the one hand, you appreciate Mrs. L.'s desire to be independent and her right to decide for herself. On the other hand, you are aware of the real risk of injury. Also, you think that Mrs. L.'s family may sue the facility if she is seriously injured. Her daughter has been upset about the falls and wants her mother to be protected.

Mrs. P.— You agree with Mrs. M. that the walker is necessary. You feel that she should get used to the walker now, before her condition gets worse.

H-4

RESIDENT CHOICE IN NURSING FACILITIES

The list below suggests some key areas for involving residents in decisions which affect them. It is not exhaustive; residents may want choice in other areas. Also some residents will not want to make decisions in every area.

Treatment

Who will be his/her personal attending physician.
When to talk to the attending physician.
What are the goals of treatment.
What treatment procedures will be used.
Whether to be transferred to a hospital.

Daily Care

When to wake up and go to bed.
When to eat.
What to eat.
When to bathe/shower.
Which activities to participate in.

Other Aspects of Daily Living

Who to sit with in the dining room.
Who will be his/her roommate.
How to decorate his/her room.
When to close the door to his/her room.
When to leave the facility to shop or visit.
When to have alcoholic beverages.
Whether to smoke.
When to use the telephone.
How to manage his/her money.
What contact to have with family and friends.
What contact to have with outside groups (such as a church, club, ombudsman).

H-5

VIGNETTES: FREE CHOICE

1. Mrs. R., chair-bound after a hip fracture, refuses physical therapy, but she loves to go to the twice–weekly bingo game. To encourage Mrs. R. to receive the therapy, the nurse in charge of her care says that she must go to therapy if she wants to be taken to bingo.

   Does Mrs. R. have free choice in this situation?

   _____ Yes _____ No

2. Miss S., a frail but alert resident, has a lump in her breast. The procedure and its risks (minimal) have been explained to her and the risk of not having the biopsy has also been explained. However, she does not want to have the biopsy because she is afraid of the procedure. The social worker talks to her in order to convince her that the biopsy is a minor procedure with low risk. She also offers to accompany Miss. S. to the clinic where the procedure would be done.

   Does Miss S. have free choice in this situation?

   _____ Yes _____ No

3. Mr. B. is quite frail and needs assistance in many activities of daily living. He cannot dress or bathe himself without assistance, needs a wheelchair to get around, and needs someone to cut up his food. He depends on the help of nursing assistants to carry out these activities.

   Does Mr. B. have the capacity to make decisions for himself?

   _____ Yes _____ No

4. Mrs. C. has spent her life helping and nurturing others. She has never cared for games, crafts, or physical activity. Today's activity schedule at her nursing home includes armchair exercises, making holiday decorations, and card playing.

   Does Mrs. C. have a meaningful choice of activities?

   _____ Yes _____ No

H-6

FACULTY GUIDE INVOLVING RESIDENTS

Activity Two: Vignettes, "Free Choice" (10 minutes)

Hand out "Vignettes: Free Choice." Ask students to read the four vignettes and answer the questions. Then discuss each vignette. The following commentary suggests main points to raise.

Vignette 1: Mrs. R. does not have free choice in this situation. The nurse is using control over going to the bingo game as a way to force Mrs. R. to receive treatment that she does not want.

In this case, there is a threat of punishment, but it would also be coercive if the nurse promised Mrs. R. a special reward for going to therapy. The nurse is probably doing this out of genuine concern for Mrs. R.'s well-being, since the physical therapy is important for rehabilitation. However, it would be more appropriate to try to persuade Mrs. R. to freely consent, as in the next vignette.

Behavior modification uses rewards and/or punishment to encourage desired behavior. From an ethical and legal perspective, it is only appropriate if it is *desired by the person whose behavior is being changed.*

Vignette 2: Most people would agree that Miss S. does have free choice, at least if she has been given adequate information about the risks and benefits of the biopsy and its alternatives. This is an example of an effort by the social worker to negotiate consent for a procedure which she or he considers to be best for Miss S. The process of negotiating consent is examined later in this unit.

Vignette 3: Mr. B. still has the capacity to make decisions. Bart Collopy (1988; 1990) makes a distinction between "decisional" autonomy and "autonomy of execution." "Decisional" autonomy is the ability and freedom to make choices. "Autonomy of execution" is the ability to carry out those choices. In long–term care, many residents are able to make choices but must depend on others to help carry them out.

In Collopy's terms, Mr. B. can exercise decisional autonomy if his caregivers give him the chance to make choices about how he wants them to dress or bathe him, where he wants to be taken in the wheelchair, and when and what he eats.

H-7

Often, caregivers who are responsible for carrying out the daily care needs of residents like Mr. B. also make the choices about how to do so. They may believe that Mr. B.'s frailty also affects his mental capacity. Or they may just assume that Mr. B.'s dependency gives them the right to make decisions for him.

Vignette 4: None of the activities available to Mrs. C. is likely to be meaningful to her. A choice is meaningful if it allows the person to express and develop his/her own values and preferences. According to Agich (1990), a person must identify with a choice in order for it to enhance his/her autonomy. To a vegetarian, a choice between a sirloin steak and a pork chop is no choice.

The students may suggest possible choices that would be more meaningful to Mrs. C., like helping to read to residents with limited vision or serving on the resident's council. It may also be possible to involve Mrs. C. as a helper in one or more of these activities, to support her desire to be helpful.

H-8

FOCUS: NURSING IN LONG–TERM CARE SETTINGS

Patient Rights/Advocacy
Regulatory Agencies and Legislation

Required Preparation:
  S & L: Chapter 3, Public Policies and Issues
       Appendix I, Community Resources

Supplemental Preparation:
  R & B: Review Unit 6 as needed

Key Concepts:
  ethics
  rights
  legality
  advocacy

Student Objectives:
  1. Define ethics and legality. Provide examples of each kind of decision.
  2. Discuss the rights retained and/or forfeited when a person is admitted to a long-term care facility.
  3. Explain what a living will or durable power of attorney for health care is, and how one is created. Identify who may and who may not be witnesses to one.
  4. Discuss issues of obtaining informed consent from elderly clients.
  5. Suggest strategies for nurses to be advocates for particular client groups, such as the elderly.
  6. Demonstrate effective advocacy for individual or groups of clients in the long-term care setting.
  7. Discuss the effects of Medicare, MediCal, and Title XXII on long-term care facilities and residents.

H-9

Thought Questions:

1. What are the most pressing ethical dilemmas you have observed in long-term care? How do you think these should be handled?

2. What is the appropriate role for an associate degree registered nurse in advocacy for clients?

Appendix I
Syllabus (Excerpt)
The Nursing Home Clinical

I-1

THE NURSING HOME ROTATION

The nursing home clinical experience is designed to assist the student to better understand the scope of nursing practice in long–term care. Emphasis is on development of individualized outcomes for residents, on management of a large group of residents with cross–model chronic health problems and on the creation of a therapeutic milieu for residents in a chronic setting. The nursing home rotation is four weeks in length.

Week I

Focus: The Unique setting of the Nursing Home

Objectives:

1. The student will describe the therapeutic milieu of the nursing home.
2. The student will discuss the philosophy of the nursing home setting, the care vs cure orientation to delivery of services.
3. The student will orient to the physical surroundings of the nursing home and organize groups of residents according to student teams.

Suggested Topics to be Discussed:

1. Roles of nurses and health care workers in LTC; comparison with the acute care setting, i.e., medical model vs nursing model of care delivery.
2. The setting: understanding the environment and culture; valuing maintenance goals; emphasis on rehabilitation and restorative goals; pace of care delivery; home–like environment, room arrangements to foster personalization of space.
3. Common Nursing Diagnoses in LTC; types of common health problems; emphasis on functional and cognitive assessment rather than pathology.
4. Demographics of elderly presently living in the nursing home.
5. The role of the nursing assistant in LTC.
6. Beginning therapeutic relationships with residents (four weeks in length).

Methodology:

—Orientation of students by nursing home staff and faculty.

I-2

—Students will not assume direct care activities on Day I but will choose groups of residents according to student teams and physical layout of facility. Students will organize and plan the remaining three weeks according to teams. Students will negotiate plan with nursing home staff.

—Discussion in post-conference of focus topics.

—Faculty begin discussion about the group experience **(Week III)**.

Week II:

Focus: The Individual in the Nursing Home: Functional and Cognitive Assessment

Objectives:

1. The student will perform a complete assessment on selected residents to include a functional assessment (agency tool), a cognitive assessment (Folstein Mini–Mental Status Exam), and an assessment of affective status (Geriatric Depression Scale).

2. The student (and student teams) will utilize the nursing process to develop a plan of care to restore and/or maintain functional and cognitive ability of the older adult.

Suggested Topics to be Discussed:

1. Use of standardized tools.

2. Polypharmacy and its effects on functional and cognitive ability.

3. Impact of chronic illness on adaptive functional and cognitive ability of older adults; differentiate normal aging process from pathology.

4. Common losses in older adults and their impact on cognitive function; dementia vs depression (pseudodepression).

5. Nursing Diagnoses: Self–Care Deficit and Altered Thought Processes; how to individualize nursing interventions to restore and/or maintain function to elicit active participation of residents.

Methodology:

—Students utilize standardized tools: Functional Assessment Guide (agency), Folstein & Geriatric Depression Scale. Students report findings to team members and to total group (post-conference).

—Role–play by faculty on administration of tools.

—Students work with student teams to write care plans for selected groups of residents with emphasis on individualized goals and nursing interventions.

I-3

Week III:

Focus: Group Activities: The Resident within the Community of the
    Nursing Home

Objectives:

1. The student will identify coping styles of residents that enhance positive adaptation to life in an extended care environment.
2. The student (or student teams) will participate in a minimum of one
   therapeutic group activity with residents.
3. The student (or student teams) will plan and present a minimum of
   one educational program with staff (Week III or IV).

Suggested Topics to be Discussed:

1. Environmental influencing factors in the Nursing Home, i.e., attitude
   of caregivers
   role of the family members
   group activities
2. Inservice for Nursing Assistants; theories of teaching–learning. How
   long should it be? What is essential information? How can the nursing
   assistants be included in the planning?
3. Advocacy of the Frail Older Adult; Interventions to deal with combative residents; Reduce noise and environmental stresses.
4. Treatment Modalities to restore cognitive function: groups (remotivation reminiscing), validation therapy.

Methodology:

—Post-Conference Discussion of Environmental factors; examples of
   unique experiences of residents (how do residents describe the setting?)

—Student development and/or participation in group activities, i.e.,
   exercise, current events, intergenerational groups, music, games, reminiscing, sensory–stimulation.

—Inservice for NA's by students on a specific topic.

I-4

Week IV:

Focus: Termination of a Long–Term Therapeutic Relationship

Objectives:

1. The student will repeat the therapeutic group activity from Week III.
2. The student will evaluate the impact of termination of a therapeutic long–term relationship with an older adult.

Suggested Topics to be Discussed:

1. The impact of termination on the client: Another loss?
2. The impact of termination on the caregivers: NAs, LPN.
3. Continuity of care: Strategies for continuation of care plans.
4. Self-rewards in long-term care.
5. Empowerment of staff in long-term care.
6. Self-evaluation: What have I accomplished? What can nursing accomplish in long-term care?

Methodology:

—Each student report in post–conference on their time spent with an individual resident in the nursing home. How did that interaction lead to a therapeutic outcome? How has this activity been an empowering experience for the student. (Allow each student a chance to "tell their story")

—Invite staff to post–conference.

I-5

SUGGESTED READINGS & FILMS:

Nursing Home Clinical

Week I: 1. Hahn, A. (1970, August). It's tough to be old. *American Journal of Nursing,* 1698–1699.
2. Millard, S. (1989, December). The ending place. *Nursing and Health Care,* 559–562.
   The Unique Setting of the Nursing Home
3. Video: Perspective of Hope (Produced by the Robert Wood Johnson Teaching Nursing Home Project).
4. Whall, A. (1988). Therapeutic use of self. *Journal of Gerontological Nursing, 14*(2), 38–39.

Week II: **Functional and Cognitive Assessment**
1. Benison, B. (1986). Aging and movement therapy. *Journal of Gerontological Nursing, 12*(12), 8–16.
2. Brady, P. (1987). Labeling of confusion in the elderly. *Journal of Gerontological Nursing, 13*(6), 29–32.
3. Hall, G. (1988). Alterations in thought processes. *Journal of Gerontological Nursing, 14*(3), 30–37.
4. Iverson-Carpenter, M. (1988). Impaired skin integrity. *Journal of Gerontological Nursing, 14*(3), 25–29.
5. Milde, F. (1988). Impaired physical mobility. *Journal of Gerontological Nursing, 14*(3), 20–24.
6. Nesbitt, B. (1988). Nursing diagnoses in age-related changes. *Journal of Gerontological Nursing, 14*(7), 6–12.
7. Penn, C. (1988). Promoting independence. *Journal of Gerontological Nursing, 14*(3), 14–19.
8. Rader, J., et al. (1985, July–August). How to decrease wandering, a form of agenda behavior. *Geriatric Nursing,* 196–199.

Week III: **Group Activities: The Resident within the Community of the Nursing Home**
1. Burnside, I. (1986). *Working with the elderly: Group processes and techniques.* Boston: Jones & Bartlett.
2. Chaisson-Stewart, G. (1985). Planning a therapeutic environment. In *Depression in the Elderly.* New York: John Wiley & Sons.
3. Janssen, J., et al. (1988). Remotivation therapy. *Journal of Gerontological Nursing, 14*(6), 31–34.
4. Slimmer, E., et al. (1990, January–February). Helping those who don't help themselves. *Geriatric Nursing,* 20–22.